Far from Russia

Far from Russia

Russia

A MEMOIR

Olga Andreyev Carlisle

ST. MARTIN'S PRESS ✖ NEW YORK

THOMAS DUNNE BOOKS.
An imprint of St. Martin's Press.

FAR FROM RUSSIA: A MEMOIR. Copyright © 2000 by Olga Andreyev Carlisle. All rights reserved. Printed in the United States of America. No part of this book may be used or reproduced in any manner whatsoever without written permission except in the case of brief quotations embodied in critical articles or reviews. For information, address St. Martin's Press, 175 Fifth Avenue, New York, N.Y. 10010.

Portions of this book, in different form, have been published in the *New York Times*, *Solzhenitsyn and the Secret Circle* (Holt, 1978), and *Under a New Sky* (Ticknor and Fields, 1992). Quotes from *Poets on Street Corners* (Random House, 1980) reprinted by permission.

Design by Nancy Resnick.

Library of Congress Cataloging-in-Publication Data

Carlisle, Olga Andreyev.
    Far from Russia : a memoir / Olga Andreyev Carlisle.—1st ed.
      p. cm.
    ISBN 0-312-25245-5
    1. Carlisle, Olga Andreyev. 2. Russian Americans—Biography. I. Title.
    E184.R9 C37 2000
    973'.049171'0092—dc21
    [B]   99-054319

First Edition: March 2000

10 9 8 7 6 5 4 3 2 1

For my friend Inge Morath
and for my nieces Zoe, Elena, and Anya,
with love

Contents

I wish to thank my husband, Henry Carlisle; my agent, Gloria Loomis; my editor, Melissa Jacobs; and my friend Nancy Pickering for their patience and their support.

PART I

Paris

The bell towers are ringing
Somewhere in the Kremlin
Somewhere in my homeland
Somewhere

—Marina Tsvetayeva
  (translation by Olga Carlisle)

CHAPTER ONE

The Sound of Poetry

My earliest memories are of adults reciting poetry in our apartment near Paris—my father, my aunts and uncles, and Marina Tsvetayeva. I would have been five or six, and I did not know that there were worlds beyond our family, the darkening dining room, the hot fragrant tea, and the waves of poetry that engulfed us.

Tsvetayeva had pale green eyes, her skin was swarthy, and her short hair was touched with silver. I liked her harshness—the brisk movements, the low, slightly raspy voice with the hard r's of the well-born Muscovite.

Tsvetayeva wore heavy silver bracelets on her wrists; a leather belt was drawn tightly around her waist. I remember her sharp profile against the twilight, the clinking of her bracelets and the Russian verse delivered in a somewhat stylized manner, vibrant and yet even toned.

This was also how my father read poetry, and my aunt Ariane, who knew all of *Eugene Onegin* by heart. Some years later I would be told that, according to his contemporaries, Pushkin had recited poetry in this way.

I had been told that Pushkin had been Russia's greatest poet, that he was being celebrated just then in 1937, on the centenary of his death in a duel, secretly plotted by the Russian Czar. Pushkin's poems and Lermontov's, the other great poet killed in a duel, were often read at the table after dinner. The adults were divided: my aunt Natasha and my grandmother preferred Lermontov to Pushkin, but the others, including Tsvetayeva, favored Pushkin.

I too considered myself a Pushkinite, although it was Pasternak, yet another poet, who was in fact my favorite. Though he was hard to understand, it was he who spoke most beautifully about Russia, the faraway land of summer woods, of lilacs and swirling snow-storms. My father read his poems with special fervor, causing each line to resonate. Many years later, hearing Robert Lowell read his own verse and Yeats's, I had a sense of recognition. Here in another language was the incantatory monotone with which my childhood had reverberated.

In Paris in the thirties there was a small Russian literary milieu, and my family was part of it. My parents' friends were the poet Tsvetayeva, the philosopher Berdyaev, and whenever he visited his family in Paris, Isaac Babel. These writers, unknown in France out-side a small circle of Russian readers, are now celebrated in Russia. But then, with the exception of Babel, their names were reviled in the Soviet Union, as were those of my two grandfathers, who both had been mortal enemies of Lenin.

There were many other Russian émigré communities in France in those years of different political or religious persuasions. Paris alone was said to be home to three hundred thousand refugees from the Bolshevik revolution. However, my family's loyalties were above all literary. And populist. The people, the well-being of people everywhere was a concern often discussed with the children. As were the history of Russia and her fate under Communism, about which little was known until the astounding drama of the Great Purges unfolded. By then I was seven.

I understood that we were neither Red nor White, that we "be-longed to the people." Both my grandfathers had been grandsons of serfs in prerevolutionary Russia. Leonid Andreyev, my father's fa-ther, was from the Orel region in central Russia, and my mother's adoptive father, Victor Chernov, from Saratov, on the Volga River. Both men had loathed the czarist regime, both had been revolution-aries in very different ways. Divorced from my grandmother, Cher-nov, now living in Prague, had been a leader of the Socialist Revolutionaries, the ill-fated SR party destroyed by the Bolsheviks in the aftermath of the October 1917 coup d'état. As for Andreyev, he had died in exile in Finland in 1919. He was a celebrated writer until the Bolsheviks erased his name from Russian literature.

Andreyev had been sympathetic to the SRs, and yet he was aware of the ambiguities of their political credo. Until 1908, they had condoned individual terrorist acts directed against highly placed officials. At that time the czarist regime was becoming ever more repressive. A secret "Combat Organization" within the party plotted the killings of leading czarist politicians, guilty in their eyes of intolerable crimes against the people.

But these high-minded, seemingly experienced revolutionaries had allowed themselves to be infiltrated by the Russian Secret Police, the Okhrana. Eventually czarist double agents were themselves staging some of the assassinations, settling personal vendettas and helping discredit the revolutionary movements. Arrests and executions multiplied. These inspired Leonid Andreyev's most powerful works, which explored the morality of using terror against autocracy: *The Seven Who Were Hanged, The Governor, Darkness.* . . . His visionary novella *The Red Laugh* foretold the horrors of the oncoming wars.

In the mid thirties my parents received a shipment of objects that had come from Leonid Andreyev's house in Finland. Among them was a set of bronze candlesticks and a massive Empire inkstand, which looked to me like a diminutive funerary monument. Small black steps lead to an urn that concealed a glass container of ink. Evidently writing in ink was the key to immortality. In my mind this inkstand was a sacred object, and I loved to draw it, trying to capture the bronze steps with a deliberate, ascending zigzag line.

The shipment from Finland, my father's legacy, included a vast collection of photographic glass plates. They were color transparencies. Each was mounted in double: they were meant to be viewed through a stereoscopic viewer. They had been packed in shiny flat cardboard boxes labeled in Leonid Andreyev's energetic, rounded handwriting. We had no viewer, but my father would show them to me by holding them up to the light. Their colors were lifelike, muted, and yet vivid. I was told that these images were obtained through the chemical use of potato flour. It seemed hard to believe. How could these butterfly wings glowing against the daylight come from potatoes?

Through these photographs my father's childhood became a part of mine. Sitting on the stairway, my father was the beautiful boy, with the sad, soft gray eyes—he had lost his mother when he was five. His small brother, Daniel, in a canvas summer hat, looked even sadder. Now they had a handsome, self-satisfied stepmother who tried vainly to look lovable in her pictures, clutching bouquets to her bosom. Leonid Andreyev was there too, enigmatic, sorrowful, wearing strange costumes. Close enough to touch were the visiting relatives, the Nordic landscape edged with clouds, the birch trees and the ponds shining softly. And the field flowers identical to those my mother gathered into bouquets for me to draw.

Several outsized charcoal drawings had also arrived from Finland. Among them was Leonid Andreyev's "Devils Trimming their Nails," inspired by Goya. For a while my father pinned this study in the hall of our small, sunny apartment in Le Plessis. The devils were repulsive; my mother and I hated them. Eventually they were rolled up and disappeared under the couch in my father's study, where paintings and drawings were customarily stored. I was not happy with this arrangement. In my opinion the devils, who looked both contrived and evil, should have been thrown out of our house altogether.

But in fact this picture was emblematic of what was going on in the larger world just then—the Spanish civil war, the rise of Stalin and that of Hitler. Andreyev's writings and especially his novellas remain alive today. His plays are performed in Russia after a seventy-year-long interlude. The problems Andreyev pondered are today's problems—war, violence, hunger.

How I wished there would have been photographs preserved also from my mother's childhood! She had grown up in Italy on the shores of the Mediterranean, among lemon trees and climbing roses. At fourteen in 1917, at the beginning of the revolution, she returned to Russia with her family. After the Bolshevik coup d'état she and her mother and sisters were arrested. A price was put on Chernov's head—he had gone into hiding. The women's situation was desperate. Then a friend, a former SR once married to Maxim Gorky, Ekaterina Peshkova, obtained a permit from Lenin himself for them to emigrate.

My family's adventures in revolutionary Russia had been fantastic, full of odd coincidences. They haunt me to this day. There were tales of Red Army men in pointed helmets riding through the sun-flower fields of Saratov, led by their mythical chieftain, Chapayev. Tales of night searches by the Cheka, the Bolshevik Secret Police. Denunciations and arrests in snowbound Moscow, train rides through endless frozen steppes. And the story about my mother and her twin sister, Natasha, living alone in the woods for a whole summer.

The four women in our family—my grandmother and her three daughters—were brilliant storytellers. My grandmother was the most accomplished. Some years after glasnost came to Russia in the 1980s, leafing through a volume of recollections by SR women imprisoned by the Bolsheviks on their way to Siberia and annihilation, I came across a testimonial about my grandmother's powers as a storyteller. She had an ability to bring to life whatever she recounted; be they daily events, history, plots out of Dickens or Alexandre Dumas, or events from her happy childhood on an estate in the south of Russia. In a Pskov prison, according to one of her comrades, her tales had kept her cell mates distracted for hours from the grim realities before them. Though she was an excellent journalist and a superlative cook, storytelling was my grandmother's magic gift—she was the Scheherazade of our family.

Snatched out of that grim Pskov prison thanks to Peshkova's intervention, my grandmother was reunited with her daughters and sent out of Russia to France. My maternal family's years in Russia during the revolution—where my grandfather was called from his Italian exile to be Minister of Agriculture in the provisional government that replaced the czarist regime to become a fugitive in less than a year—made a breathtaking, intricate tapestry of tales. Against it our French life unfolded peacefully. I was in awe of these tales, yet to me the present was even more compelling.

CHAPTER TWO

An Émigré Childhood

In the early thirties, my family settled in a distant, pastoral Parisian suburb. To me then Paris, some ten miles away, was like a shimmering island just out of reach. Paris was-full of unnamed pleasures—I would have given my life to share in them. This was the era of Edith Piaf, the beloved French chanteuse. On spring nights her songs played on the radio, filling the air of the housing development where we lived. Piaf's songs with their mixture of joy and anguish reminded me that Paris was close by and yet inaccessible.

Le Plessis Robinson, newly built and somewhat antiseptic, stood at the edge of a beautiful old park whose eighteenth century manor house served as a town hall for the new settlement. The park had been closed to the public for decades. However, everyone in our extended family—which included my grandmother, her three daughters with their husbands and children—knew how to climb over the crumbling stone walls that enclosed it. The park was our realm. No one ever disturbed us there, yet our intrusions were a clear violation of the established order. They marked us as rebels, as Russians.

As a family, we were different from anyone else in Le Plessis. We were younger—in those years even my grandmother was in my eyes a young woman. Our family was well educated and nonconforming—my parents called that being *intelligentnii*. Yet, as impoverished foreigners, we were outcasts rather than rulers in the world in which we lived. But within the park we were sole masters.

Every day in the good season we spent hours in the old park of Le Plessis. We picnicked there, and read poetry, and took walks along its overgrown alleys. There in the fall we looked for mushrooms and chestnuts. But even on spring days when the park was leafy and the ground covered with a thick carpet of diminutive blue hyacinths, I was never completely happy there. My thoughts were elsewhere. I was in love with Piaf's companion, the dreaded apache, the outlaw of her songs, who was hiding somewhere in Paris. The apache was the soul of Paris, dangerous perhaps, but beautiful and free. He was a hero to the French movie-going public, a star, evil and yet seductive.

Walking along Le Plessis's wide, straight avenues one could see here and there glued to the walls life-size movie posters of the apache from the lower depths of Paris. He had arrogant black eyes and wore a striped sailor's shirt and a *casquette*, a snap brim cap. I longed to see him, but I went to Paris seldom, and always with my parents. The apache was invisible except on the half-torn posters, which would soon be taken down altogether.

Even though the apache remained out of sight, my rare excursions into Paris were memorable, especially those in my father's company. From the age of five or six he took me to poetry readings at the café la Coupole, where once a month the young Russian émigré poets of Paris gathered. There I was given vanilla ice cream in a tall silver dish. I listened to sonorous Russian poems recited by my father and his friends, young men with intense faces who conversed with me as if I were a grown-up.

Settled in a back room of the café, they read their own poems and those of their elders in Paris, like Marina Tsvetayeva and Georgi Ivanov. For the most part they themselves were very young. They revered the poets who had stayed in Russia—Anna Ahkmatova and Serguei Yessenin and my favorite, Boris Pasternak. His Russia was all about youth and love:

> *At dusk you appear, a school girl still,*
> *a school girl. The sunset a woodsman hacking*
> *in the forest of hours. I lie back to wait for dusk.*
> *At once we are hallowing; back and forth we call.*

You ran across the street, winds billowing,
a flying carpet—sleds, crystals headlong!
For life inspired by the blizzard gushed
like blood into a crimson cloud.

When they spoke to me the young poets, my father's friends, used my name and patronymic, Olga Vadimovna. I was flattered, it made me feel grown up. Still my attention drifted. I was thinking about the stranger in a casquette lurking somewhere nearby, perhaps even looking for me. Seductive as Russia was, I wanted to go to Paris, I wanted to break away from my Russian world, to run toward the Seine, toward the bridges whose reflections turned the river into a many-ringed hand. Only the thought that, should I flee, I might never see my father again kept me sitting quietly in my corner. I loved my father even more than the apache. And so I settled back and tried to follow poems I did not understand, but which were full of hypnotic power whenever one allowed them to carry one away.

Years later, just before I met my husband, Henry, a stay in the United States left me again longing for Paris. It seemed to me that I was always being taken away from my native city—to the island of Oléron in the Atlantic during the Second World War and more recently to the United States, where my father had gone to work for the United Nations. There, before coming home to Paris— forever, I hoped—I had spent a year on a scholarship at Bard, a small college on a cliff above the Hudson River.

Bard had an arts department where I rediscovered my life's avocation. I would become a painter. From my earliest years in Le Plessis, I had drawn pictures. Some were suggested by my grandfather's inkwell, others by flowers, still others by the stories read to me and especially by the adventures of King Arthur's knights.

Drawing had been a way to stay in the present, escaping the past—my parents' past in Russia—as well as the future, which they hoped would take us back there. For me, it was a way to communicate with Moscow, with my uncle Daniel, Leonid Andreyev's second son—younger than my father by three years. On several occasions I had sent Daniel pictures of my heroes, King Arthur's knights, and they had reached him despite the fierce censorship imposed in those years by the Soviet authorities.

At Bard, in addition to taking a beginner's course in painting with a dynamic, imaginative instructor named Stef Hirsch, I studied English. It was taught by a handsome young Texan, Bill Humphrey. He was reserved and yet wonderfully passionate about literature. In his class we studied several American novels—*Light in August, The Bostonians, Moby-Dick.* These had revealed America to me, or so I thought, with its opposite worlds, the Yankee and the Southern. *The Grapes of Wrath,* which I had read in translation in France, had given me the desire to go west, but I would never do this, I thought. I was in America for only a year.

For I could not live in America. In 1950, Senator Joseph McCarthy held Americans under his spell. Wherever one went, people were reluctant to speak to each other openly. If they learned of one's Russian origins, they recoiled. The FBI might be on their doorstep the next day, asking them questions, probing their loyalty to America. In my experience only Bard, a liberal arts college organized along the precepts of John Dewey, appeared immune to this fear. Everyone there discussed everything as if McCarthy did not exist—psychoanalysis, Marxism, and the future of the world, which was full of hope now that the War had ended. A young professor there, a new arrival from Belgium, Paul De Man, taught the writings of Jean-Paul Sartre and Albert Camus. De Man was blond, blue-eyed, with a childlike smile. He seemed a bit secretive, but his courses were both accessible and erudite. Decades later it appeared that he was a Belge collaborator in flight from his country's justice, but no one suspected him then. I enjoyed hearing the then fashionable existentialist French vision of the world put forth by De Man. John Dewey's vision, taught in another class, struck me as decidedly pedestrian.

Some of my schoolmates were war veterans, older than the rest of the students by four or five years. They treated me with comradely deference because I was a foreigner. Several were from Jewish families, from New York and Los Angeles, and they went on to leave their mark on the contemporary theater—Peter Stone, of *1776* fame and Ted Flicker, one of the founders of the Theater in the Round.

They and my newfound love for the English language made it hard for me to leave Bard at the end of the school year, but I was missing Paris. Though my scholarship at Bard was renewed, I would go back to Paris and enlist in the Faculty of Letters at the Sorbonne. With my knowledge of Russian and my newly acquired English, I could hope to graduate from its first year's course without additional studying. This would give me time to learn how to paint.

When I returned home in January 1952, Paris was freezing and yet festive. In the bakeries there was now as much golden, crusty bread as one wanted. The outdoor markets, long empty after the war, were overflowing: they smelled of celery and of fresh fish. There were bunches of anemones and tulips, scarlet oranges from Morocco, as well as a variety of apple, gray and smooth, called *reinette*. Walking through the markets, one chatted with the merchants, bargaining a little and discussing the weather. In those years Parisian men were openly admiring yet protective of young women. I liked their good-natured flirtatiousness, it made me feel a part of Paris.

For the first time in my life I was living inside Paris. And living alone, or almost. My suburban adolescence had been haunted by the deadline of the last Métro, although I could on occasion spend the night in Paris at the home of my school friend, Aline Pagès. Now I had my own room with a separate entrance at the back of Aline's parents' apartment. It was near a park in the thirteenth arrondissement, on the fifth floor of a stylish, balcony-laced gray building dating back to the nineteen hundreds. This was a neighborhood where many exiled Russian revolutionaries had lived before the First World War. The Chernovs once rented a flat on nearby rue Gazan.

As an infant my aunt Ariane had been taken to the park in a baby carriage. An armada of Russian nurses gathered there in the afternoon with their charges including Leon Trotsky's small son, my aunt's exact contemporary. Now French children shepherded by their mothers played there: nursemaids were a thing of the past.

My friendship with Aline had begun in 1946. Right after the war, when I had returned with my family from Oléron to Le Plessis, I had been lonely. It was hard to go back to school after an interlude of almost five years of adult wartime adventures. These had involved us with the people of Oléron, who had been our close friends, my father's companions in arms within the local resistance. Now, however, we were outsiders again, Russian émigrés.

Then one day in a physics class at the Lycée Marie-Curie I sat next to Aline, and my life was transformed. Aline was a plump, energetic blonde, rebellious and intelligent, a future scientist. At fourteen she knew exactly her vocation: she would become a physician. We were both bored by the often tedious, formal French education methods of those days. The lycée became easy to bear in the company of a like-minded friend. Aline was the first close friend from a French family that I ever had.

Aline introduced me to her circle of relatives and friends, children and grandchildren of French physicists with well-known names in the world of science—Joliot-Curie, Langevin, Perrin. Much to my satisfaction, the patron saint of that milieu had been a woman—of Slavic origins at that. In the early part of the century Marie Curie, the discoverer of radium, had been awarded the Nobel Prize in physics twice. Little by little, Aline's family of intellectuals, cultivated, diffident, somewhat insular, adopted me and my parents as well, those engaging, eccentric Russians with the correct left-wing political views and no French connections whatsoever.

To be part of a group of young people my own age was exhilarating. For three successive summers, in 1946, 1947, and 1948, Aline's parents invited us to vacation near them in an isolated part of Brittany, west of Saint-Brieuc, called Larcouëst. I was sixteen and seventeen when I was slightly infatuated with one of Aline's first cousins, who was witty and a little distant and had a face like an Italian Renaissance page. Peacetime had returned to France, and France and the future belonged to us, *les jeunes*. In his memoir, *Les mots*, Jean-Paul Sartre describes the peculiar sense of being propelled with enormous velocity within a permanent present that marked that era. Was it a way of escaping from the still-burning memories of the war—a certain kind of mass-induced optimism inherited from the totalitarian spirit that had dominated much of Europe in the preceding decades?

Back in Paris that winter in 1952, I saw my French friends again, but to my surprise my infatuation with them had disappeared. Was this because of my recent discovery of a larger world? Or my determination to become a painter? I knew that this decision would disappoint my friends, who hoped that I would one day become one of them, *une scientifique*. I kept it a secret from everyone except Aline and her brother Olivier who, the year before, had chosen to study sculpture in the face of his family's anxious puzzlement.

Aline's parents' apartment on rue de la Cité Universitaire smelled of beeswax and was filled with old country furniture and thick scholarly volumes written by grandfathers and great-grandfathers who had been celebrated professors at the Sorbonne. No street sounds reached it—the apartment overlooked the Parc Montsouris, a perfectly preserved turn-of-the-century park, just as the stately elms and straight alleys of our park at Le Plessis were a legacy from the eighteenth century. Montsouris was serene even in bad weather, with its fragrant hemlock hedges and the ornamental oval pond reflecting the pale winter sky. The flowerbeds around it, dotted with deep blue pansies even in the winter, reminded one that spring would reach Paris before long. The park would fill with children, with exuberant plantings, and no less exuberant foreign students from the nearby Cité Universitaire, who had replaced the Russian exiles of past years.

I had never been happier than during the months I lived at Aline's parents'. I could do anything I wanted all day long. This had never happened to me before even though the years on Oléron had been blessedly school free. Now McCarthy's ravings in distant America no longer mattered to me, the political nightmare ever present in my family faded away. I all but stopped thinking about the contradiction between my father's love of Russia—his faith that life was improving in the Soviet Union, his desire to live there as soon as possible—with what was actually happening under Stalin and which he refused to acknowledged. Every week books that told the truth were published: *Darkness at Noon*; David Rousset's *L'Univers concentrationaire*; the defector Kravchenko's autobiography.

Early on, right after the war in 1945, we had received a letter from my uncle Daniel Andreyev. He had survived the war and had been among those who had helped lift the nine-hundred-day siege of Leningrad by the Germans. This was the first news we had of Daniel since 1939. This initial letter was welcoming the prospect of our family's return to Russia. My father knew this letter by heart; it had given fresh meaning to his life.

Within our family, otherwise so united, my father's unwillingness to believe that the war had not put an end to Stalinist terror had led to periodic confrontations. My mother, the daughter of Russian non-Marxist Socialists who had been all but eradicated by the Bolsheviks, understood perfectly. Yet, not to upset my father, she remained silent as he and I shouted at each other across the dining room table. My mother's silence saddened me. I felt that it was my obligation to wake my father up from his dream, but I only succeeded in upsetting everyone. At the age of ten my brother, Sasha, saw himself as a Russian patriot and a Communist. Our family was split into two ideological camps—my mother and I on one side, Sasha and my father on the other.

But in the winter of 1952 at Aline's, I forgot about labor camps in the Soviet Union and war in Korea. I no longer even read newspapers. In any case they were too expensive for my minuscule budget. My parents who were now settled in New York sent me a little money every month—enough for transportation, for coffee and cherries, for a few art supplies. Although Aline's family made me feel welcome whenever I wished to have supper with them, in the evenings I usually put on my best emerald green sweater and went out to have dinner with Russian relatives or with French friends.

At long last I lived in the present, a Parisian present. Every morning I walked to the Louvre, where celebrated paintings kept in hiding during the war were being cleaned one by one and put on display. Here were Giorgione's *Concert Champêtre*, Delacroix's *Femmes d'Alger*, and Cézanne's large still lifes with apples, known to me until then only from reproductions. Back at Aline's in the afternoons, I painted. The smell of turpentine, the sight of paints in their little lead tubes made me dizzy with delight. In my own mind I was learning to paint still lifes. I was trying to understand what it was that made Cézanne's so exceptional. Inspired by them, walking home from the museum, I often bought apples, or a spiky artichoke, or a fish. I painted these right away. Afterward, Jeanne, the family cook, put them to good use in the kitchen.

My room at Aline's opened through a French door onto a bal-

cony, which skirted the entire apartment above the treetops of
Montsouris. Nestled behind its decorative cast-iron railing, I could
sketch the Parisian skyline beyond the park. Just below me the
brown buds on the bare chestnut trees were growing bigger and
shinier. In my room by the balcony door, where the light was strong-
est, Aline's brother Olivier had set up an old easel, which had belonged to his mother. Here I worked.

In those years I especially liked the paintings of Soutine, who
had been an acquaintance of my father's before the war. My realistic
still lifes were coarsely painted, yet once in a while, miraculously,
one would become alive with shapes and colors. On such days, life
truly seemed worth living, but this happened seldom. More often
than not I was in a state of mild distress over my artistic failures.

Whenever I was particularly disheartened I tried to forget about
painting altogether. I stayed in my room at Aline's and read all day,
slowly, the random volumes of Henry James that I had brought
back from America. I sometimes found the plots difficult to follow,
but this only made the novels more interesting. I could withdraw
from my Russian and French worlds and take refuge with Isabel
Archer and the Prince and Charlotte and Maggie. I was in the
company of people so much more complex and devious than anyone
I had ever known that I found it hard to stop in the evenings to
visit with Aline or to go out. Sometimes I thought I would see
Henry James's heroes strolling in the distance in turn-of-the-century
Montsouris, visitors from a turn of the century America possessed
by greed and a lust for decorum.

CHAPTER THREE

Americans in Paris

O n the *Liberté*, which had brought me back from America, a young woman, a friend of my parents who was also aboard, introduced me to a very thin, very tall American of twenty-four or twenty-five. His name was Robert Gilkey. Gilkey spoke extremely fast, with a trace of a British accent, and he wore well-cut tweeds. He had a sardonic smile and affected Old World manners—he had lived in Europe before. Now he was returning to Paris from Philadelphia to defend his doctoral thesis at the Sorbonne.

I knew at once that Gilkey was a cynic: while paying all assiduous court to my parents' friend, he was attentive to me as well. I soon realized Gilkey needed someone to help turn his lengthy, ungrammatical French text about Mark Twain's *Innocents Abroad* into a thesis acceptable to the august Sorbonne for a *doctorat d'université*. When we reached Paris, Gilkey was calling me at Aline's and inviting me to dinner, trying to coax me into editing his thesis, which was due at the university that very spring.

I too was a cynic: I accepted Gilkey's invitations though I had no illusions as to his motives. I knew no other American in Paris, and though Gilkey's French was fluent, he was willing to speak English with me. All of a sudden I was seized with nostalgia for Bard and especially for the English language. Like my childhood Russian—and unlike French, which is all rules and intricate constructions—English flowed freely, releasing fresh feelings and ideas whenever one spoke it.

Gilkey, my one American acquaintance in Paris, lived in a fine old apartment in the heart of the Latin Quarter on rue de Cluny. His windows opened onto the archaeological site near the Cluny Museum, from which the Roman emperor Constantine's baths were being excavated at that time. The procedure, carried out by two or three elderly workers in dusty blue overalls, picks in hand, had an unwitting kind of solemnity. It was so slow, in such contrast with the nearby boulevard Saint-Michel, where crowds of students milled up and down endlessly, laughing and speaking every possible language. Some of them were Americans.

Overhearing them, my thoughts went back to America. Had the ice on the Hudson River begun to break up? In Paris, spring was making itself felt in the smoky mild air. Just a year before, in the company of a thoughtful World War II veteran who was studying psychology at Bard, I had walked along its banks in the moonlight. We kissed. That night the Hudson was beginning to thaw out in a huge commotion of thundering ice floes. Perhaps I should have taken on the challenge of America? I could have stayed on at Bard, or gone on to nearby Vassar, where I had been offered a scholarship in exchange for courses in beginner's Russian.

From my perspective, Gilkey's existence on rue de Cluny was positively baronial. He had a maid who cooked dinner and served it by candlelight in a dining room furnished with diminutive eighteenth-century furniture upholstered in faded brocade. Though Gilkey had his thesis foremost on his mind, he appeared not to want to force the issue of my helping him with it. We had long conversations, about American literature. Gilkey worshiped Mark Twain but found Henry James bloodless.

It was about an hour's walk to Gilkey's house from Aline's. Whenever I was invited there, I would find a new route through the gray stillness of the thirteenth arrondissement, along rundown workshops and fenced-in gardens, which had stood outside the city one generation before. I savored these late afternoon walks through a section of Paris unknown to me until then and yet oddly familiar—perhaps my childhood love, the apache, lived there? Some of the inhabitants of the thirteenth, the workers in casquettes who clustered at dusk in the small cafés on my way, looked a little like he.

Gilkey gave cocktail parties, and I was pleased to be asked. No one else I knew in Paris served whiskey and canapés at the end of the day. I liked the well-being induced by a drink of scotch and the intense conversations on literary and political subjects. Here too was an excuse to wear my party dress, a green-and-red plaid one, with a round white collar that made me look like young Colette, or so I hoped.

Gilkey truly came into his own whenever he gave a party. Animated, affable, speaking quickly, he went from group to group, sharing with his guests the latest bit of Sorbonne gossip. Or else he recounted elaborate, somewhat enigmatic stories involving the covert activities of certain Americans throughout the world. This was the age of the "Ugly American," but no one seemed to know what it was that this American was actually doing. Was he upholding democracy or trying to subvert progressive political movements outside America? Was he a cunning businessman? Or perhaps he did not exist at all, an invention, a spoof? I for one had never met him, in any guise.

At his parties, Gilkey assiduously introduced his guests to each other—he had made sure that among them there was a happy balance between pretty girls, influential Sorbonne professors, and American expatriates like himself. I especially looked forward to meeting the latter, with whom I might perhaps continue, in English, the conversations begun in earnest at Bard, about the future of the world.

Gilkey's maid, a small gnarled peasant woman from Brittany put on a black dress and a lacy white apron on these occasions. As if by magic she was transformed into a stylish *femme de chambre*, her urbanity matching that of the host. Candles were lit throughout the apartment even before darkness fell, and trays of hors d'oeuvres set out. A mixture of French and English was spoken at the gatherings, which lasted well into the night. Sometimes celebrated Sorbonne professors such as Gaston Bachelard and Jean Wahl were in attendance in the furthermost salon of the apartment, where two sofas were upholstered in dark green velvet and the windows looked straight out onto the Cluny gardens.

The expatriate contingent at Gilkey's parties was made up of young Americans who were studying philosophy or literature at the Sorbonne. Others worked as translators or were poets. An Englishman named Arnold Fawcus had just started a small publishing house based in Paris. Trianon Press would publish art books whose reproductions were to be printed by hand in the Jura Mountains, where craftsmen expert in the art of fine printing could still be found.

Fawcus had been one of the founders of the American military ski units in World War II. He was a short, truculent man, older than Gilkey by a good ten years. In a loud, heavily accented French he complained about his estranged wife, who lived in England and made unreasonable financial demands. Arnold paid court to Gilkey's female friends by being rude to them. No one I had ever met had done this—but then Arnold had served in the OSS and had parachuted behind enemy lines, capturing single-handedly a German regiment during the Battle of the Bulge: His brashness was that of a seasoned warrior.

One evening at Gilkey's, settled on one of the green velvet sofas, I was listening to Professor Bachelard, an academic luminary who was the author of a study on the poetics of fire, which was much admired in Paris in those years. Outside, the Cluny gardens were turning a dark blue. Bachelard, elderly, stout, had a fan-shaped beard that covered his chest. He wore a starched collar, which looked as if it had been cut out of cardboard. He punctuated his words with wide, mellow movements, discoursing with the easy fluency of the French intellectuals of the old school who were becoming extinct just then. Bechelard was one of the survivors of pre–World War I France, when Frenchmen were happy with themselves, confident in the ultimate goodness of France and of the world.

Two or three young people were listening to the professor respectfully. I was struck by one of them, an American. For a moment I liked everything about him—his blue eyes and very dark hair and his air of natural nobility, which made him stand out in the small Parisian salon. He was tall, he could be one of Henry James's visitors from America, one of the uncorrupted ones. But right away I felt distrustful. Brought up in a Latin country, I assumed that a man as good-looking as this could only be conceited.

Moments later Gilkey introduced Henry Carlisle to me. He was a poet living in Paris and working on a scholarly study of French prose poems. This intimation of academic dedication lessened my distrust a little, and we had an exchange about the respective attractions of Paris and of his native San Francisco. Henry said that he did like Paris, but preferred San Francisco, a seaport with a mild, Mediterranean climate—despite its summer fogs, roses and bougainvilleas flower there year-round. Had I ever been to the Midi, he asked? I hadn't, and yet once, long before the Russian Revolution, my mother's family had lived on the Italian Riviera for several years. Henry explained that he had spent part of the previous summer on the Côte d'Azur. "It's bright and full of life and just as luminous as California," he said.

CHAPTER FOUR

Boissia

I saw less of Gilkey in the weeks that followed. He was becoming frantic about his thesis, yet I was determined not to undertake its editing at the expense of my own work. I had been brought up in a Chekhovian world where the women, even though quite gifted themselves, were self-effacing, promoting their husbands' talents at the expense of their own. On the other hand, when I was eleven or twelve, during a heart-to-heart conversation, my father had assured me that, in his opinion, women, though sometimes lacking in will-power, were otherwise no less gifted than men. Encouraged by this, I was determined to take my work seriously. I felt sorry for Gilkey but kept ignoring his pleas for help.

After a long silence, one day in April, Gilkey telephoned to invite me for a weekend in the Jura Mountains. I accepted, although our host would be none other than the truculent Fawcus himself, who was restoring a château near the Swiss border. We would drive through Burgundy in Fawcus's convertible. It was to be a true holiday—few of my friends had cars then, and none had castles.

But on the eve of our departure Gilkey called again. As far as he was concerned the expedition was off. He had alluded to her on occasion—Sylvia, the woman of his life, a Spanish aristocrat who might be leaving her husband for him—had just arrived in Paris. He could not go anywhere at this crucial moment. However, Fawcus had suggested that I could come alone if I wanted. Ever so slightly stung that Gilkey would give up a house party in my company for a weekend with a Spanish aristocrat, I told him that I would go to Fawcus château without him. I could perfectly well take the truculent Arnold in my stride.

The next morning a huge silver-gray Mercury convertible drew up to the door of Aline's house. The car was what the French called then *une belle Américaine*. Arnold Fawcus was at the wheel, red faced and looking very pleased. A French couple in their thirties, unknown to me, were settled in the back of the car. Next to Arnold sat Henry Carlisle. He was even more handsome than I had remembered.

Fawcus drove like a madman—fortunately in 1952 there were few cars on the French roads. Heading southeast at eighty miles an hour, the Mercury swayed like the *Liberté* herself. I sat in the back of the car, wedged between Fawcus's French friends. The Vuittons were well-dressed, in sports clothes that came straight from Hermès. Clearly they were members of the French bourgeoisie, a class of people against whom I was prejudiced though I had had few occasions to encounter them outside of novels. In this response to the Vuittons I was conforming to my French friends' convictions, who were Socialists and freethinkers in the nineteenth century, anticlerical Sorbonne tradition. My own family, though made up of Socialists, held no preconceived notion on such matters, always welcoming encounters with new people.

The Vuittons owned a country house near Marcus's château. On this particular weekend they would be his houseguests—the following day we would all go skiing in the Jura Mountains. More noticeable even than their expensive clothes was the Vuittons' intense dislike of each other. Filling the back of the car like a malevolent fog, it expressed itself in hissing exchanges that could not be overheard by those sitting in front.

From the driver's seat, glancing backward altogether too often for our safety, Fawcus carried on in a booming voice about brainy females who forget that women think with their ovaries. He had recognized a feminist in me, although I was hardly anything of the sort in those years. On the contrary, it seemed to me that my being a woman rather than a man was inadvertent, an accident, a disguise perhaps. Though limiting at times, this was not without interesting possibilities, but being teased by Arnold Fawcus was not one of these.

Quite irritated, I sat in silence between the Vuittons. Suddenly to my amazement I felt a hand behind me. Deliberately, slowly, Mr. Vuitton was caressing my lower back. I shifted my position, I leaned forward, but he was not to be discouraged. In fact, he became more insistent while continuing to argue with his wife about family finances. Now I was angry: here we were, barely a hundred kilometers out of Paris, and while Arnold Fawcus was accusing me of thinking with my ovaries, his French bourgeois friend was fondling me against my wish. Not looking at Mr. Vuitton, I tugged at Henry Carlisle's sleeve. I was a little carsick, I said. Would he mind changing seats with me?

For the rest of the trip, as we raced across Burgundy at dizzying speed, I sat next to Fawcus. To try to divert him from his pleasantries I asked about his publishing house. Taking on occasion his hands off the wheel and waving them to make a point, he described the ancient silk-screen methods still used in certain towns in the Jura Mountains to create reproductions of watercolors virtually indistinguishable from the originals. A new facsimile edition of William Blake's hand-drawn *Jerusalem* was to be his first publishing adventure.

We reached Fawcus's château, Boissia, by midafternoon. Darkness was beginning to fall upon a landscape of small stone villages scattered among meadows buried in snow. The foothills of the Jura looked bleak. Thinking of the bouquet of anemones that Aline had given me and which I had not had time to paint, I was distressed. Seduced by the notion of châteaux and of convertible cars, I had involved myself in a tiring, unnecessary adventure.

With its pointed tiled roof and smooth gray walls, Boissia looked stylish and severe. Once, in the fourteenth or fifteenth century, it had been a fortified manor. Later on it had been used as a farm. Evening was coming as Fawcus took us on a tour of his domain, around the massive stone walls and down a muddy path to the vegetable garden half buried in snow.

Inside, Boissia was in a state of extreme disrepair. There was nothing intimidating about the first château I was visiting as a houseguest. Only a few of its cavernous rooms were restored. Broken columns, a crumbling fireplace could be made out in the dark. As we stumbled up and down unlit stairways littered with fragments of

stone, Fawcus was outlining plans for the rebuilding of Boissia—
they were grandiose.

The château was fiercely cold—survival was foremost on our
minds. A fire was lit in the big cooking stove of the half-restored
kitchen: we all joined in an emergency operation—kindling and old
newspapers were found in the kitchen and half-frozen logs carried
up from the courtyard. Even the Vuittons good-humoredly participated. Mme. Vuitton, a vivacious brunette, was flirting with Arnold.
Her husband—tall, aristocratic, vaguely distraught looking—was
signaling to me his wish for a few words in private. Perhaps he
wanted to apologize for his impertinence? I ignored him with all
possible discretion. I was terrified at the idea of being caught between the warring Vuittons.

Once the fire was going and boxes of groceries brought in from
the vast trunk of the Mercury, Arnold took everyone upstairs. We
toured the second floor, where he assigned us our respective rooms.
The Vuittons were given a bedroom right above the kitchen. Located next to a bathroom, which would be getting hot water from
a tank connected to the kitchen stove, it might eventually warm up
a little. Henry's room beyond it, furnished only with a double bed,
was freezing. Mine at the end of a very long vaulted corridor was
even colder. It too had a large ancient-looking wooden sleigh bed
as its sole furnishing. This however was the room with the best
view, Fawcus said. The high gothic window, now tightly shuttered,
looked toward the mountains where we would go skiing the next
day.

While the Vuittons went up to their room to freshen up and to
continue fighting—their angry voices could be overheard despite the
thickness of the walls—Arnold disappeared and then reappeared,
proudly carrying a big plucked chicken, a present from the peasants
who looked after the château in his absence. Then he took a bottle
of marc, the potent local aquavit, from one of several imposing
armoires which stood around the kitchen. Between the fire which
now crackled and the marc, Arnold, Henry, and I were thawing out.

I was about to take off the ski jacket which I had borrowed from
Aline for the trip. Just then, looking sly, Arnold said, "Don't take
your jacket off yet, Olga, old girl. I need some leeks to go with my
chicken. Here's a flashlight. Why don't you dig us some while Car-

lisle and I peel the potatoes? Near the stove over there, you'll find the shovel. You know where the vegetable garden is. There is a row of leeks on the left as you go down."

I was a believer in the equality of the sexes, yet in the world in which I lived women stayed in the warmth of the house peeling potatoes while men went out to dig in the snow. I said in an unnaturally clear voice, "Arnold, why don't *you* go, or ask Henry? I'll be happy to peel potatoes."

Fawcus roared with laughter. He declared once again that women think with their ovaries—and only about how best to take advantage of men. At that moment Mr. Vuitton came into the kitchen. He picked up the shovel eagerly. Would I light his way into the vegetable garden? Instead, I handed the flashlight to Henry. He was smiling, evidently he found Fawcus amusing. I made an effort and returned his smile. Obligingly, Henry led a disappointed Mr. Vuitton into the frozen depths of the garden in search of leeks.

Fawcus's chicken took forever to cook. As we waited for dinner we tasted a whole variety of Burgundy wines, red and white. Some had been brought by the Vuittons, others were taken out of one or the other of the kitchen armoires—four or five of them that were standing around the room. Fawcus and the Vuittons were talking about the difficulty of restoring old manor houses. Though the French government was allocating funds to qualified owners, the local peasants were rarely persuaded to work to that end. For reasons unclear to Fawcus and the Vuittons, though remaining polite they managed always to decline this kind of employment. "All they like to do is climb up on their tractors," Fawcus said disapprovingly.

When the chicken was ready at last, he proved an enthusiastic host, carving it with a flourish and pouring out more wines. These were beginning to make me sleepy—I was the first to go upstairs. In the huge room with only a bed in the center, I undressed quickly and laid down, wrapped tightly in my robe. There was a heavy old quilt atop the bed which kept me warm—I fell asleep immediately.

I woke up with an icy nose. I had been dreaming about my childhood island, Oléron. I was walking along its wild shore with my father and Sasha. The pebbles at my feet were covered with ice and sparkled like the sunshine that came in through the cracks in the shutters. On the beach I had felt very free. It was with a sense of sorrow that I found myself alone in a dark, freezing room.

Remembering what Fawcus had said about a view, I got up and with a great effort pushed open the wooden shutters closing the gothic window. A landscape of fields and towering black rocks stretched out before me, looking as if it had been painted by a Zen monk. A range of pale blue mountains could be barely made out on the horizon. All around, the silence and the cold were over-powering.

Downstairs the kitchen was warm—the big stove had not gone off at night. Arnold was making coffee and giving curt orders to everyone. If we were to have time on the Jura slopes we were to leave immediately, as soon as we had selected skis from the vast collection that stood against one wall of the kitchen. That I was the last to get up was not lost on my host: clearly I was a *lazy* feminist.

That morning the Vuittons seemed to have had a reconciliation, yet as we were loading skis onto the Mercury, Mr. Vuitton pressed into my hand a piece of paper with his telephone number written on it. I settled in the back of the car at a safe distance from him. By noon, climbing steadily, we reached an immense snow-covered plateau, where the sun was blinding and the wind blew hard. Beyond it, a rounded, fir-covered mountain was slashed with a narrow ski run. Alongside it there was a rope tow that seemed to be leading straight to the sky. Here we parked and put on our skis.

Fawcus became another man as soon as he put on skis—suddenly he was a patient and soft-spoken instructor. Teaching skiing had been one of his avocations during the war. He led me to a hillock nearby and gave me a lesson keyed to my beginner's abilities. Then while I practiced, he took on Mme. Vuitton, who kept falling into the snow and laughing coquettishly. Using the rope tow, Henry and Mr. Vuitton had disappeared from sight.

It felt good to move in the snow. The altitude, the sunshine lifted the tensions of the last twenty-four hours. After a while, feeling a bit light-headed, I sat down in the snow and watched Arnold give Henry a skiing lesson. Henry followed Fawcus's instructions with effortless precision. Briefly he looked at me from a distance and smiled a luminous, unexpected smile.

We picnicked right there in the snow—we had white burgundy wine and gruyere cheese and a dark peasant bread, which we had bought on our way to the mountains. Though the snow still sparkled, the shadows of the fir trees on the mountain were lengthening and turning a bright purple. It was time to go. On our way back to Boissia we dropped the Vuittons at their house. It suited them, a pretentious Victorian manor decorated with turrets and a fake moat in the middle of a small mournful mountain town. As they disappeared across the wooden bridge that straddled the moat, Fawcus declared that the Vuittons were the crème de la crème in that part of Jura. As far as I was concerned, they had only confirmed my low opinion of French bourgeoisie.

Now Fawcus and Henry were speaking English about the future of Trianon Press, a subject which absorbed Fawcus. I felt exhilarated, it had been a marvelous day. Henry was smiling at me, he too looked contented. I loved his sudden smile, which contrasted with his usual reserve. At twilight as we neared Boissia, the black rocks towering about the snowy fields created an atmosphere of mystic tranquility.

The stove in the kitchen of the château was still warm, and we revived it and turned our thoughts to making dinner. Once again Fawcus disappeared, saying as he left, "Now, Olga, old girl, don't you flirt with Carlisle here while I am out: Gilkey entrusted you to me!" I wanted to protest, to explain that my friendship with Gilkey had never been anything but comradely, that he had stayed back in Paris to be with a Spanish aristocrat. But protestations would only have spurred Fawcus on, and so I restrained myself and said nothing.

When Fawcus disappeared Henry suddenly said, "As a matter of fact I would love to flirt with you, if you don't object." I was embarrassed but also pleased. I said, "Yes, let's . . . ," but then I asked him about skiing in California, in places where people live by the sea and yet, even in summertime, are only a short drive away from snowfields.

Soon Fawcus returned in triumph. This time his neighbors had given him a jar of magnificent mushrooms. He would make us a mushroom omelet. While he cooked with extreme concentration, chopping onions and parsley and grating cheese, Henry and I talked quietly. Henry told me about his work on French prose poems. I liked the unpedantic yet intense manner with which he spoke. Were the outward calm, the composure innate or the result of his upbringing? What lay behind the humorous restraint? Surely Henry had a great love of literature, and that put me at ease.

As we ate, Fawcus told us how during the war he, an Englishman, was called to California to teach American troops to ski. Then Henry told about his family background. All of it was maritime. His mother came from a long line of American naval officers, his father's ancestors were whaleship owners and merchants from the island of Nantucket. I tried to describe my wartime years on the island of Oléron. Our islands on opposite shores of the Atlantic had to have certain similarities, although Nantucket is covered with moors, whereas Oléron is a land of vineyards.

After dinner I washed the dishes and went to bed at once. I was falling asleep when I heard a light knock on the door. I sat up and switched on my lamp. Henry stood in the doorway. He was wearing a dark red tasseled bathrobe, which was perfectly suited to the gothic decor. He came up to my bed and took my hand. "Why don't you join me in my room?" he said. "I'll keep you warm."

I knew that I had flirted with Henry, but I was not aware of having done anything to elicit such a straightforward invitation. Nor had his own manner prepared me for this. I said, "No." Henry's face changed, his eyes turned black. I looked at him and thought he was the most attractive man that I had ever met. I was seized with a mixture of delight and panic. For an instant I had the impression that I was becoming someone else as I said, "All right," and got up and followed him barefoot into his room.

CHAPTER FIVE

Rue de Seine

P aris was even more festive when I returned from Boissia. Spring
had come to the city. The trimmed treetops of Montsouris
formed a smooth green carpet below my window at Aline's. The
light in my room had changed: it now was tinged with pink and
even harder to capture in paint. I spent hours in the park drawing
trees. I tried to seize with pen and india ink that moment of spring
when the leaves are still so small that a tree's structure is visible, yet
the overall aspect is one of softness. Sometimes Aline came down
to the park with me. We sat down and talked in the dappled sunshine while I drew with a mixture of pleasure and rage—no matter
how hard I worked, my drawings were disappointing.

In the evenings I put on my green sweater or a clean blouse and
went out to have dinner with Henry Carlisle. Walking to the Quartier Latin, I noticed that Piaf's songs were once again filling the air
of the sections of Paris that I crossed—the thirteenth, the fourteenth, where workers still lived in those days. Piaf was back, but
without the apache. She was now in love with a famous boxer who
loved her back, yet her songs were still warning that love is full of
dangers. I was unconcerned, I was falling in love with Henry.

Henry lived at 31, rue de Seine, quite close to the river, in the
back of a massive eighteenth-century apartment house. A recipient
of the GI bill and therefore affluent by the standards of those days,
he rented a flat on the top floor. His windows looked upon a sea
of silver gray roofs watched over by the bell tower of Saint-Germain

des Prés. Chopin and George Sand were said to have lived in that house at the beginning of their love affair.

Henry's apartment on the seventh floor was made up of three garret rooms: a kitchen lined in ancient, chipped tiles with a carved stone sink; a dining room with a round table and a smelly gas heater, which Henry treated without concern, despite my admonitions—stories of deaths caused by faulty gas heaters abound in Parisian lore; and a bedroom with an old iron bed that had a deep depression in its center. There Henry and I made love whenever I visited him.

I loved our lovemaking, despite the creaky bed and the fact that we were both quite inexperienced, something we tried to conceal from each other. Although he had been in the navy just before the end of the war, Henry's life had been sheltered; he was fastidious by temperament. As for me, all Parisian that I was, I was far from precocious. Throughout my childhood, my parents' invigorating, Scandinavian-inspired nudism had had a distinctly inhibiting effect on me. Later on as a teenager during the war, though not especially pretty, with my dark hair and green eyes I was striking looking. Wishing to go about unhindered, I trained myself to be inconspicuous. Censoring my comportment I also censored my impulses. But now on rue de Seine, little by little, I was freeing myself from restraints.

That spring in the old iron bed, lovemaking was taking on another dimension for me. It was linked to that one pleasure that I valued above all others, the pleasure procured by the opulent, golden paintings that I singled out in the Louvre. Paintings such as Giorgione's *Concert Champêtre*, which I had first seen there as a child before the war and never forgotten, and Titian's voluptuous *Nude with a Mirror*. Eroticism and painting were interrelated in my mind, and each made the enjoyment of the other more intense. The secret of lovemaking was in letting oneself be led by one's body, fingers and lips taking over and finding beauty. Painting also had to be like that, the soft touch of the brush a caress.

Henry too seemed in love, though he said as little as possible on the subject. He was as anxious as I to avoid a pregnancy. I knew that he wanted to keep a distance between us and I found this quite acceptable. I cherished the freedom that Paris had given me. None-theless I found myself to be the one seeking greater intimacy. This made me melancholy at times, but then I had been brought up among people immensely involved with each other and with the events of the times, the mood set by poets whose hyperbolic lines I knew by heart:

> *Werther has already been written: today*
> *To open a window is to slash one's veins.*

To expect people who weren't Russians to share or even to sym-pathize with this kind of poetic fervor would have been foolish. I assumed that I would never encounter it outside my family, since our country, Russia, was lost to us.

Henry was the most beautiful man I had ever met, and the most enigmatic. It was his reserve that attracted me. I never quite knew what lay behind the courteous manner, the blue eyes that had a way of turning dark. Henry was moody in ways and for reasons that kept eluding me, though I tried hard to decipher these.

From the beginning books were a bond between us. We usually agreed on literary matters, though our tastes far from coincided: Henry favored Joseph Conrad, I, Henry James. Henry's literary in-telligence, his critical sense were all the more remarkable considering he had grown up in a family oblivious to the very existence of literature. He had discovered books at sixteen when he read Kafka's *Trial* by accident: a writer he had spoken to casually one evening in a restaurant in San Francisco had praised it to him, and he went out and bought it.

We agreed on literary matters but argued about everything else. Henry's politics were moderate and quite reasonable, while the rad-ical in me would often spring forth during a conversation. Perversely, I allowed myself to revert to my adolescence. As a teenager I had read about the French Revolution and had been inspired by the rhetoric of the Jacobins, of Robespierre and Saint-Just. I had wanted to think that the world could be transformed all at once through a revolution, a belief I no longer held but one that I enjoyed parading on occasion in the face of Henry's sensible views.

If I asked casually about a woman, "What does she do?" it sounded provocative to Henry. Women kept house and raised children and discreetly furthered their husband's careers. To expect them to have a profession of their own was in poor taste. Yet paradoxically Henry was respectful of my desire to become a painter. Once in a great while he did remind me that easel painting was a thing of the past, that other art forms would soon replace it. I agreed that this might well be so, though it saddened me to think that I was working in an outmoded discipline. I hoped that perhaps Henry was wrong, but of course he has been proven right: Conceptual art has superseded painting.

Henry had an innate sense of form—in manners, in clothes, in literature. He could say at once whether a painting was good and if not, why, as if he had known all about painting in another life. I sometimes brought my pictures over for him to critique. Yet while literature engaged him completely, he remained unaffected by painting. He almost never went to museums. My attempts to persuade him to come to the Louvre with me usually failed.

More often than not, our disagreements were diffused by a perfectly timed, amusing remark from Henry. I loved his wit, dry and quite unlike my family's gentle, pervasive sense of humor. He made it clear that in his opinion I took life too seriously. Henry used his wit to dismiss situations that might otherwise have become distressing. Fighting back the familiar habit of what the French call *aller au fond des choses,* "getting to the bottom of things," I tried to go along—here was a proved, entertaining way to avoid arguments. My only regret was that I was unable to respond with remarks as amusing as Henry's. But even if I had been as witty as he, the sense of threat created by repressed disagreement would have stopped me.

Through Henry I was discovering a point of view on life that was more detached than anything I had ever thought possible. Perhaps my father and Camus were wrong, and it was not necessary for each of us personally to take responsibility for the world? Perhaps it was naive to believe that it was within our power to improve the fate of people around us? Clearly my passion for painting was selfish, I was not serving humankind by drawing trees or apples.

I would have liked to converse forever with the handsome, diffident visitor from America, who knew things about which I had no idea. Henry understood how money affects people, he knew about personal plays of power and about family manipulations. These were situations I had encountered both in books and in life but had never really probed. I had my way: in addition to the delectable times in the bed with a deep depression in its center, Henry and I spent hours talking in English: Henry's French was as good as my English, but he willingly gave in to my desire to speak English. He enjoyed teaching me American expressions that I found incongruous and charming, like "having egg on one's face," "put the show on the road," and certain navy sayings that came from his mother's family: "three sheets to the wind," for inebriated.

We talked in small student restaurants, some of which offered *steak frites* and a beer for a few francs; in more elegant ones like the Coq d'Or, near the Panthéon, where the Russian cooking was authentic and the fairy tale decor inspired by Chagall cast a spell that two or three glasses of wine intensified. In the late afternoon we talked at the terrace of the Brasserie Saint-Germain, where American expatriates gathered that year. Or else we would stop by the more stylish Brasserie Lipp. There we ran into Gilkey and into Fawcus who made obscene jokes about my love affair with Henry.

Things had not worked out for Gilkey and the Spanish aristocrat. He was still looking for bilingual young women to help him with his thesis. There were two or three who appeared in turn in his company at Lipp's. Gilkey was more restrained than Fawcus, yet he was not above implying with a chuckle that I had slept with him before meeting Henry. This bothered me, but when I tried to say something on the subject, Henry laughed, and said something like, 'Qui s'excuse, s'accuse.' Your past doesn't interest me. Before I know it, you'll be asking me about *my* past. Now as a matter of fact, there was a pretty nannie when I was five years old . . ."

What I liked best were dinners in Henry's apartment *en tête-à-tête*. Rue de Seine was the best place of all to talk, and Henry sometimes cooked exotic, fragrant dishes such as curries, which I had never tasted before. I had not known that men, other than professional chefs, could cook. Once in a while I tried to reciprocate. I would prepare one or another of my mother's family's specialties in the kitchen, which looked like a Bonnard print with the chipped blue tiles and the window overlooking a sea of silver roofs. Sometimes I made Russian meatballs, or ratatouille, for which I brought the ingredients.

On my way from Aline's to rue de Seine, I would shop for our meal. I bought bread at the corner of Boulevard Saint-Germain and rue des Saints-Pères in what was said to be the best bakery in Paris. It was a spacious, old-fashioned shop decorated with black glass panels embossed with golden garlands. Their, croissants were tightly packed on wicker trays, and baguettes stood guard on tall gilded shelves. Their ranks were decimated through the day, but fresh recruits appeared and disappeared again as evening neared.

I bought vegetables at the open market on rue de Buci, rich with noises and smells. It was patronized by the inhabitants of the *quartier*. Women in cotton smocks and felt slippers and men in caps stopped there after work. They were filled with reverence for the task at hand, selecting the very best asparagus, persuading the butcher to part with the tenderest lamb chop. On rue de Buci at around six o'clock, the end of the shopping day, one could buy small bunches of violets and baskets of strawberries from the Midi for almost nothing. There *reine de Mai* from Cavaillon, the most opulent of early lettuces, cost one franc.

After dinner at his apartment, Henry and I often went out again into the spring night. We walked to the Seine nearby and looked at the dark water slowly flowing by. Then we stopped at the Café des Beaux-Arts on Quai Voltaire for coffee and more conversation, only to go back to rue de Seine and fall into bed. What happened afterward was the one serious subject of contention between us in those days. Henry insisted that I stay and spend the night with him. I would decline. This interfered with the next day's work, and painting was the goal I sought to put ahead of everything else. Moreover I suspected that, in the mornings, the apartment on rue de Seine became a great deal less romantic than it was at night.

I would try to persuade Henry to get dressed and take me back at least partway to Aline's: He was reluctant to let me go and to let me go on my own, although Paris at night was safe in those years, and I liked long night walks alone. More often than not we went together as far as the Gare du Luxembourg. From there the last train for Cité Universitaire left just short of one o'clock in the morning.

CHAPTER SIX

Parisian Tulips

June came. On place de Furstemberg, off rue de Seine, where
Delacroix had once had his studio, four small trees that had
looked dead suddenly sent forth huge clusters of white blossoms.
The gates of the Luxembourg gardens were left unlocked late into
the night, and their moist darkness smelled of lindens and cut grass.
On our way to the Métro, we sometimes made a detour and looked
at Notre Dame in the moonlight. It had stood there for almost nine
hundred years, an astonishing poem in stone, a promise of permanence.

Fate caught up with me one evening at the Café des Beaux-Arts.
Henry and I were sitting there after dinner holding hands when two
familiar, bearded figures walked in. They were Aline's brother Olivier and his friend Jean-Pierre, who were students at the Ecole des
Beaux-Arts around the corner. They affected the Parisian artist's
costume of those days—paint-splattered corduroy trousers, French
berets and an air of profound contempt for the bourgeois world
around them. I had no choice but to recognize them and introduce
them to Henry. I Henry asked them to join us, a bit stiffly—he was
shy under his elegant aloofness—the miraculous anonymity of my
love affair was shattered.

For I had not mentioned Henry to Aline, or to anyone else for
that matter. Aline had been protective of her privacy for as long as
we had been friends. We never discussed our affairs of the heart.
Distrustful perhaps of my Russian expansiveness, Aline discouraged

confidences. My late homecomings that spring had not been mentioned. Using the side door of her parents' apartment, I had been free to come and go as I wanted.

Now, though Olivier and Jean-Pierre were polite, they were studying Henry with barely disguised disapproval. I knew what they were thinking: "An American—Olga with an American! What a pity!" I almost could hear what they would say to Aline the next day, "We saw your friend Olga in the Quartier. She was drinking beer there—in the company of a rich American!"

Hostility against Americans ran high in France in those years, especially in the left-wing milieu to which my French friends belonged. In this, secret envy for a nation victorious in 1945 played a part. The United States was seen as an imperialist power by Frenchmen oblivious of the fact that their own well-being was founded in good part on France's overseas empire, still intact at that time. Reports about political terror in Russia were dismissed as the inventions of reactionaries. Visiting Americans were intruders taking advantage of a favorable money exchange. That evening as we said good-bye to the Frenchmen after a tense round of beers, I knew that I would soon have to take a stand about Henry. I feared that not only my friends, but my parents, due any day now for a summer holiday in France, would find my involvement with him reprehensible.

We walked back in silence along rue de Seine. A full moon cast shadows along its narrow canyon. I was about to follow Henry into 31, rue de Seine, its facade shining with an otherworldly sheen, when he stopped abruptly. "I do not feel very well tonight," he said. "Let me take you right to the subway at Saint-Germain des Prés." Obviously my friends had offended him. I started to explain: "Olivier is Aline's brother. I live at their house. Aline is a close friend, I think you will like her if you ever meet her. As for Olivier and Jean-Pierre, they are like so many Frenchmen today, they like to show off in front of foreigners."

We followed the deserted streets leading to Saint-Germain. With its wooden stalls now all boarded up, rue de Buci looked ghostly. Only a faint, sour smell of crushed strawberries reminded me that this was one of the *ventres de Paris*, feeding that part of the city day after day. An Arab wearing sandals and a shabby overcoat was sweeping the sidewalk with a long broom. I saw a small tulip lying on the ground. Wrapped in its own leaves, it was intact. I picked it up and put it inside my purse. It was a parrot tulip, a silky mixture of red, white, and green. I wanted to paint it the next day. This thought diverted me—how best to paint a single tulip, a small, disheveled tulip whose petals seemed cut out of Florentine paper?

We crossed place de Furstemberg, which was filled with moonlight—it was like walking through a bowl of weightless silver milk. The four small trees in its center were still laden with creamy blossoms. I reached for Henry's hand. He took mine and pressed it and then released it. I tried to comfort myself: "Tomorrow I'm sure I'll be able to tell Henry about those idiotic Frenchmen. Their sense of inadequacy makes them aggressive. It's all because of the French debacle in the last war."

The next morning I painted the parrot tulip that had opened wide in the warmth of my room. Silently, with its ragged petals spread out, it seemed to call out for help; yesterday's small tulip had become a wild flower, and it had to be painted wildly, as Soutine would have. I squeezed out some cadmium red and Veronese green and lots of white, and worked quickly. The tulip was done in no more than half an hour. I had the good sense to stop before the colors became muddy. While painting I was thinking about Henry. I knew that living in Paris could at times be hard on him. Parisian men, the ones who were nice to the girls on the street, were often unpleasant to a foreigner as tall and diffident looking as he. I noticed it when we went out together—a surly remark in a shop, a waiter who was rude. This did not happen when I was alone.

Later that day I walked to rue de Seine, bringing with me the ingredients for the Russian specialty Henry liked best, known in my family as "eggplant caviar." Henry greeted me as if nothing had happened the evening before. His headache was gone, he said in response to my question.

Since there was no oven in the small kitchen, I roasted the eggplants directly on the flame of the gas range. With a big kitchen knife I chopped them along with tomatoes and parsley. I used a chopping board made of newspapers covered with Henry's typing paper. The apartment filled with a sharp smell of parsley.

Outside, the sunset touched the gray roofs with pink—even the stern square bell tower of Saint-Germain des Prés was pink. This was the longest day of the year. We were going to have dinner and then go out for a walk along the quays. We had a glass of red wine. I mentioned something my grandmother used to tell me, about pagan midsummer celebrations in northern Russia on that one night when once a year ferns are said to come up in blossom.

Henry said, "I'm glad you are Russian. When we went off to Boissia, at first you looked to me like a French girl, a little demure. My mother has a Russian friend in San Francisco. She makes dresses for the society women there, but in reality she's from the highest aristocracy. She has the most perfect manners of anyone in the world. At sixty she is still a great beauty. Her name is Lita Ilyn— Mrs. Kiril Ilyn."

We sat down at the round table decorated with a bouquet of white tulips. With that sudden luminous smile Henry told me that he had bought them for me on rue de Buci—the previous night he had looked on in bewilderment as I had picked up that lost parrot tulip from the sidewalk.

I said, "I want to apologize for my friends last evening. They are stupid—they believe that the Soviet Union is a paradise, which America is bent on destroying. They were rude." I was thinking of my father. He of course would never be rude, yet his political convictions differed little from those of Olivier and Jean-Pierre.

"Yes, the French *are* stupid," Henry said. "Most of the century's disasters can be directly blamed on them. World War II, for instance. Had they been less vindictive in 1918, it may not have happened."

"But German militarism . . . ," I said.

Suddenly Henry's eyes darkened. "As for those Frenchmen last night, they acted as if they knew you intimately. Which one is your lover—or both?"

About to help myself to the eggplant, I put the spoon down. I wanted to get up from the table and walk out in dignified silence. Walk down the seven flights of 31, rue de Seine and never come back. Instead, I said feebly, "Neither. Neither is my lover. But I do have French friends and Russian ones too, and I love some of them dearly."

I took a spoonful of eggplant caviar. I had oversalted it. Suddenly I burst into tears. Sitting across the table, Henry looked alarmed, yet he kept silent. Now to my surprise I was sobbing. All I could think of was that spiral wooden staircase leading down and out of the house. The concierge spent her days waxing it, it was very slippery. I would have to calm down before I could negotiate it, wearing as I did high-heeled shoes. Or should I take them off first? I had to leave at once. Henry did not love me—worse, he did not respect me.

I got up from the table, pushing back my chair, which fell onto the ceramic tile floor with mournful thud. Stumbling, I looked for my purse. Henry got up too. He walked up to me around the table and took me in his arms. I did not resist as he led me toward the creaky bed in the next room.

Only later, after we said good-bye at the Luxembourg station did I remember that Henry had offered no apology for implying that I was promiscuous. As the subway purred along softly but firmly, rushing me from the Quartier Latin back into my French world in the thirteenth, I replayed in my head the scene at dinner—Henry saying in that cold, low voice: "Which one is your lover—or both?" I would only remember the lovemaking in the creaky bed which had been more delectable than ever. Otherwise I could not go back to rue de Seine—and I wanted to.

CHAPTER SEVEN

La Vie en Rose

Some days later, on an overcast Saturday morning in the company of Aline, I went down to Parc Montsouris to sketch. In a sun-dappled spot by the pond we settled side by side on a bench. I drew a willow tree whose branches almost touched the water. Aline picked up and then set aside the notes she was studying for her year-end exam—in those days the school year in France lasted till mid-July. "Olga," she said, "I have never meddled in your life, but here you are, back in France. Among your friends. Come spend part of the summer with us in Brittany. Spend more time with us."

I did not look up from my drawing, but I knew that Aline had been told about the encounter at the Café des Beaux-Arts. I did not want to discuss it. I said, "I often daydream about Larcouëst. I would love to go back there. We will make plans in a week or two, when my parents get to Le Plessis. However, there was some question of our going on a camping trip in the Midi. I have wanted to go there all my life. Perhaps you'd come with us? Just imagine, we'll be looking at some of the landscapes that Cézanne painted! My parents would be so pleased if you come along!"

Aline said that she would think about it, though missing the summer months at Larcouëst just then seemed unthinkable to her. I looked up at Aline. Her narrow, intelligent face looked concerned. With her long blond hair braided tightly and her doubting expression, my friend looked very much like the sixteenth-century pencil portraits in the museum at Chantilly, which I had seen with Henry some days before—I had managed to persuade him to take a whole day off and go there by train. Nothing was said about the encounter at the Café des Beaux-Arts, nor about my late hours in the Quartier Latin. Aline studied her notes intently while I drew the willow branches, the patterns their reflection created in the water. The day was still gray, but there were bursts of sunshine that once in a while illuminated the park and turned the water a bright green.

Aline was studying hard—she was nearing the end of her pre-med course. Before her, were another five or six arduous years in medical school. My own future looked less arduous but a great deal less well-defined. The problem was how to conciliate my love of literature with my decision to become a painter. To support myself as an artist might prove hard, while a *license de lettres*, followed perhaps by the exacting *aggrégation*, would make it possible for me to teach in a lycée for the rest of my life and still have some time to paint. The learned spinsters who were our teachers at the Lycée Marie-Curie saw me as one of them. They had told my parents with a quiver of satisfaction in their soft spoken voices that even the difficult Ecole Normale Supérieure might be within my reach: "*Elle est si sérieuse. . . .*"

But the year I spent in America had made the French university appear dull. Here was a world where no living writer was studied, where literature was all but destroyed through relentless analysis. It seemed to me that, symbolically, I would be expected to help murder a living art in order to join the ranks of those who lived off it. Painting, on the other hand, was "instantaneous forever," in Pasternak's words. Nor did it force me to choose among the three cultures that fate was offering me—the soulful, sonorous Russian one; the cerebral, challenging French one; and now the American, with its huge, uncharted riches.

Shortly before my trip to Boissia, Aline had reminded me that I had to register at the Sorbonne if I wanted to take the year-end examinations at the Faculty of Letters. On a rainy morning she had taken me there, suspecting that, left to myself, I might neglect to do it. She had guided me along a maze of corridors and dark offices crowded with bewildered-looking students. The academic formalities took hours, they were depressing, yet eventually I was allowed to take the necessary examinations and qualify for further study in the literature section at the Sorbonne.

The exams were given at the center on rue de l'Abbé de l'Epée, off boulevard Saint-Michel, where Aline and I had once taken the dreaded *bachot* (the baccalauréate) at the end of our lycée years. But this time it all seemed like a game. Sitting at a narrow child's desk with a wooden bench bolted to it, writing an essay on the portrayal of evil in Molière's *Don Juan*, suddenly I felt elated. I was taking leave of my adolescence. I would become a painter and yet remain involved with French literature. Except for the lycée's overdoses of Corneille and Racine, I did love it. Even if I had to struggle through the difficult *aggrégation* to support myself—hadn't the poet Mallarmé once been a teacher of English in a lycée?

But now looking at the swirling reflections of the willow branches in the pond, I was less certain. "Aline, no matter how hard the studying, medicine is what you love. But teaching in a lycée will always be a compromise for me. Remember how we hated the way literature was treated at Marie-Curie? The useless hours spent analyzing poor old *Andromaque*? The answer for me is right here, within the reflections of that willow tree. Except that I don't know how to deal with them," I added gloomily. My drawing wasn't developing well.

"The only answer you'll find in the water is about the world's lack of permanence," Aline said, She had a great deal of common sense: "Look at how the reflections change with the light."

"Then my vocation may be to try to capture the ephemeral, though of course I'd prefer eternity! Speaking of such things ..." I wanted to tell Aline about Henry. Making love to him was of course ephemeral, but I wanted it to last forever, it was becoming almost as important to me as painting. But I stopped.

Aline had always been critical of my interest in men, of what she called my *légereté*—as in *femme légere*, "easy woman." "You flutter your eyelashes and look at whoever turns up as if you might be his for the asking," she would say sarcastically. And it was true that, more often than not, I flirted without even knowing it.

Flirtatious or not, in those years young girls, even the daughters of intellectuals, were expected to remain chaste. I had been breaking the rules. How would I explain to Aline that, besides being a flirt, imprudently, I had allowed myself to fall in love with Henry Carlisle? That I thought of nothing but Henry all day? That I slept with him? Better say nothing at all—Aline hated confidences anyway.

I tried to concentrate on the reflections in the pond. They formed a wondrous, moving mass of mauve and green and white. I was getting nowhere, yet there had to be a way to capture them. My drawing was worthless. I tore it up. I would come back to the park when the light was more steady, tomorrow perhaps.

Just before everyone started to leave for lengthy summer vacations at the seaside—a sacred ritual for Parisian academics—I received several invitations from my French friends. This had to be an organized effort to try to reclaim me from America. I accepted the invitations, which usually included Aline. I felt bad at having seen so little of my friends since my return from the United States. It was hard for me to imagine that before my trip there my happiness had depended on such invitations.

Aline's brother Olivier, who usually paid little attention to us, the *jeunes filles*—Aline and I were five years younger than he—invited me to spend an afternoon at the Louvre with him. This too had to be part of the rescue effort. Olivier was a slender, aristocratic-looking young man, beautiful even when dressed in work clothes. He wore a short, well-trimmed beard, and his light brown eyes were speckled with green. Like his sister's, his face was finely chiseled, as in a Clouet drawing, but Olivier was more handsome than Aline, and more artistic.

When I was sixteen I had had a crush on him. I had hoped that he might invite me to one of the less risqué parties at the Ecole des Beaux-Arts. But Olivier and his friend the painter, Jean-Pierre, preferred the company of mature, emancipated young women to that of young girls. In disgust, Aline and I referred between ourselves to the women they favored as *rois de Bohème*, the "kings of Bohemia." They all seemed to have swarthy complexions and wear heavy gold earrings and drink a lot of wine. Their masses of crinkly dark hair hung down to their waists. Oblivious of our feelings, Olivier and Jean-Pierre told us in suggestive detail about the orgiastic encounters at the annual Bal des Quat'z'Arts, making it clear that such pleasures were not for us and never would be.

Now that I lived at his parents', Olivier and I had occasional conversations about art, which were drawn out and involved—Olivier had an abstract turn of mind. He was preparing for the competition of the Prix de Rome in the sculpture section of the Beaux-Arts. Recently this had meant virtual incarceration, for many weeks, inside a *loge*, an isolated cell where a young artist worked in secrecy on an assigned theme taken from classical mythology. Olivier's sculpture, just completed but not yet juried, was entitled: *The Death of Astyanax, Son of Hector and Andromache*. He explained that it was a low relief of a little boy about to be thrown off a high wall, Hector's son, killed after the siege of Troy.

Such an academic approach to sculpture seemed unpromising to me, and I sometimes said so, but so timidly that Olivier did not quite hear what I was saying. Mostly I listened—Olivier was extremely erudite. In particular he knew a great deal about the archaeology of old Paris. For years it had been my dream to be taken by him on historical tour of the city, from the Catacombs in the fourteenth arrondissement to Notre Dame and Sainte Chapelle. But it had never happened because he was busy at the Beaux-Arts. Then he had fallen in love with Hélene, whom he was going to marry against his parents' wishes.

Hélene was a secretary. Though one of the *rois de Bohéme*, she was truly beautiful. Hélene looked like Nefertiti, regal and detached, but when she opened her mouth she appeared to be a practical, prosaic individual, just what her future husband was not. For a whole year Olivier had been working on a bust of Hélene as the Egyptian queen, but in a modern headdress and with a softer mouth.

Olivier was inviting me to the Louvre at his sister's request, but I was pleased nonetheless. At the entrance of the museum, in the immense hall where the French school was exhibited in those days, we looked at the paintings by Delacroix, although Olivier favored the work of Delacroix's adversary, Ingres, whose seated *Grande Baigneuse* wearing a red turban was right there, her face averted, self-contained, monumental, magnificent. But it was with the Delacroix that I fell in love all over again, and especially with his *Liberty Leading the People*. Once, when we were away from Paris during the war, someone had sent me a picture postcard of that painting. The hazy mass of the Left Bank buildings in the background had filled me with nostalgia. Here was the inaccessible silver gray Paris of my dreams, the Paris of the apache. But now I felt that I at last possessed Paris. I could see it through the windows of the Louvre, more dazzling on that early summer day than any of the paintings within.

Olivier, who liked to instruct, gave an elaborate technical commentary about the composition of the *Femmes d'Alger*, in which Delacroix suggests masterfully an enclosed, sensuous space, that of an Oriental brothel. With a pang of regret I realized that only the year before I would have been overjoyed at spending time in the Louvre listening to Olivier speak about Delacroix. But now I was looking at my watch, I was interrupting him. I had a date with Henry at the Brasserie Saint-Germain at four o'clock.

Nonetheless, on our way out, we took time to look at *The Artist's Studio* by Courbet. There on the right sat Baudelaire in profile reading a book. I was seeing an old friend. Baudelaire, like Delacroix, was an inhabitant of my private Paris, my favorite French poet. Never had Paris looked finer, as reassuring as on that afternoon, both inside the museum and outdoors along the quays of the Seine.

We stepped out of the Louvre and crossed the river, back to the Left Bank. The good weather was holding, Paris was sunny and easygoing. Some foreign dignitary was in the capital on an official visit, and the bridges were decorated with French flags that clapped softly in the wind. I said goodbye to Olivier and raced up rue Bonaparte toward Saint-Germain and Henry. I was half an hour late for our meeting.

I saw him from a distance at the terrace of the Brasserie. He was speaking with a French poet he knew, who called himself a *lettriste*. Instead of words, the *lettriste* used only letters in his poems—words were passé, as were sentences. He was a fierce-looking young man in a black leather jacket who moved with big movements that belied a world in which letters, rather than words or sentences, mattered. Henry was listening to him attentively, looking like a visiting prince from some faraway kingdom. It occurred to me that perhaps the flags on the bridges were flying for him. He was courteous and attentive and yet unconsciously he kept the *lettriste* at a distance. Once again his aloofness made him irresistible, it made me want to find the key to him.

That morning a letter from my parents announcing their arrival from New York at the end of the following week had come. I planned to tell Henry about it. My parents and my brother, Sasha, would come home to Le Plessis and stay there for several months. The four of us would be going to the south of France for a vacation, to the Mediterranean where I had never been. To a region where it never rained in the summer and the sea was warm. Although this would mean a temporary loss of freedom, I was delighted. I missed my parents. I had never before been separated from them for very long.

When the pallid young poet said good-bye and I sat down and ordered a crème, Henry told me that he had just written a poem, which he wanted me to hear right away. It was about the island of Nantucket. At Bard, reading *Moby-Dick*, I had been overwhelmed: here was America's *War and Peace*, the anatomy of whaling like that of military strategy in the Russian novel, a stubborn study of a discipline now obsolete but which had once held together a society. It was wondrous to think that Henry's people had been whaling men on Nantucket, that two of them had been portrayed by Melville.

In Henry's poem, inspired in part by the French prose poems on which he was working, the island was a state of mind rather than a place. Carefully spreading the typewritten page on the marble table, Henry read it out in a low, warm voice. It was a dialogue between a boy and his grandfather, a Quaker patriarch of Nantucket.

"I guess I'll be forever haunted by Nantucket," Henry said, afterward. "My father grew up there, and he never gave up his ties to New England. But I was born in California, and I am from the West through and through. In the same way you are a Parisian before you are a Russian, though in fact I often marvel how someone born in exile can remain as tied to an absent country as you are."

With Henry I always liked to be as exact as I could. "As a matter of fact," I said, "I have never quite succeeded in becoming French, although Aline and her family have tried hard to make me feel like one of them. Paris is my city, but some part of me will always belong to the island of Oléron, to the ocean there. The Atlantic there is so beautiful! The tides can be enormous. I wonder whether they are like that on Nantucket. Just beyond our house, big round waves came up to a jetty. From there at high tide we could dive right into the ocean. When the German occupation came, a femme fatale insinuated herself into our family, and I discovered that evil can be an everyday occurrence, as ordinary as getting up in the morning and eating breakfast."

"In *Moby-Dick* Melville tries to find where evil lies," Henry said. "Surely not within the white whale. No one on Nantucket thought that the killing of whales was evil, yet it troubled Melville."

"If I lived up to my convictions I would at once become a vegetarian," I said. "I'd eat only eggplant caviar and omelets and cherries."

"And baguettes with lots of butter," Henry added. "As a matter of fact, the people who slaughtered the whales, Quakers for the most part, were the more decent from among the ruthless men who founded America."

At that moment I heard six o'clock ring out at the bell tower of Saint-Germain des Prés. In a few minutes I was to meet Aline at the home of her cousin Françoise, who lived on the southwest edge of Paris. Henry invited me to have dinner with him at the small student restaurant on rue du Dragon, which we especially liked. We agreed instead to have lunch there the next day.

Henry walked me across the boulevard Saint-Germain, to the Métro on the sunny side of the street. On the broad sidewalk by the church, a young woman behind a cart decorated with pink painted butterflies dispensed ice cream. Next to it a man sold balloons. A woman who walked by was humming Edith Piaf's song:

> Quand il me prend dans ses bras,
> Il me dit des mots tout bas,
> Je vois la vie en rose . . .

We had left the intellectuals' world at the Brasserie for the sunshine of Piaf's Paris. I decided to exert a Parisienne's prerogative—Parisians kiss in the street. I kissed Henry for a long time before plunging into the coolness of the Métro.

CHAPTER EIGHT

Farewell to Henry

At lunch the following day in the student restaurant on rue du Dragon, we were eating *céleri remoulade*. I was telling Henry that my parents and my young brother, Sasha, were about to arrive. The four of us were going on a holiday. Then my father would work for the General Assembly of the United Nations, which was to take place in Paris that winter. My parents were to stay till the beginning of the following year. I was leaving Aline's parents' place and moving in with my family to our small apartment in Le Plessis. I'd come see him as often as possible on rue de Seine.

Henry asked, "Will you still be able to spend the night with me once in a while?" That would be difficult, but I could visit him in the late afternoon and stay into the evening. Might he come out to Le Plessis for dinner before we went off? My parents had decided that rather than risk rainy weather in Brittany we would go camping along the coast of Catalonia. Aline would not be coming with us. She could not bear to be away from Larcouëst where her family and her friends were once again gathering for the summer.

As I spoke, Henry looked somber. At first I thought that I had dropped some celery on my blouse, or perhaps said something in English that made no sense or was outright offensive—some of our misunderstandings came from my imperfect English. But it was not that. "Olga," he said in a firm, low voice, "I left San Francisco to escape girls who wanted me to meet their parents. I am not ready to meet your parents, nor anyone else's. Though I am sure yours are exceptionally nice. In any case, you know how busy I am. I must press on with my prose poem translations. Fawcus says that Trianon might publish them in a bilingual edition."

"But why not come out to Le Plessis late some evening?" I asked, although I knew the answer. Henry thought that I wanted to introduce him to my parents—as a prospective fiancé! It was absurd. My parents' arrival would curb my independence that summer, but there could be other carefree seasons for us. I said, "Henry, you needn't worry. My parents do not want me to marry—anyone. I am twenty-one. After our arduous years on Oléron, they want me to be without responsibilities for as long as possible. They want me to go to the university. Aline says that what they really want is to keep me for themselves. Whatever the reason, you are safe."

Henry's face remained closed. He poured us some wine and said nothing. "All my French friends have met my parents. They come to dinner at our house and stay up late and talk. My parents treat young people as equals." And suddenly I was saying things that were shocking, yet I could not stop. "We are in Paris, Henry, not in your old-fashioned San Francisco, full of heirs and heiresses and fortune hunters. You Americans think all we Europeans want is your money. For us at least things have changed since the days of Henry James."

It was as if someone else was speaking—Henry was not rich, he could not possibly suspect me of wanting to marry him for his money. Perhaps, unconsciously, I had expected him to propose to me? With each day I was a little more in love with him.

Henry said in a very low voice, "Olga, you are making a spectacle of yourself, you are shouting. What is the matter with you? You don't know a thing about San Francisco. Nor about America. Nor about me."

I made an effort to control myself. I had not realized that I had raised my voice, but evidently I had: people around us were looking up. For a while we ate in silence. I did not touch my wine. Then I said icily, "Whatever your reasons for not wanting to meet my parents, I am sure they are excellent. It is true that I know nothing about San Francisco and about your American ways. But my own ways are such that I cannot be involved with a man who will not be introduced to my family—my parents are my closest friends. So perhaps we should end our friendship right now." Realizing what I had said I added, "Or postpone it till other times."

Henry said nothing. He paid the bill and walked me to the subway in silence. We stood at the entrance of the Métro on place de l'Odéon. Danton's bronze statue gazed down on us. I said in what I hoped was a calm, clear voice, "And so good-bye, Henry. Do have a good summer."

"Good-bye, Olga. Remember, you are always welcome at rue de Seine."

I glanced up at Danton, the heroic orator of the French Revolution who had been one of my childhood heroes. Now stretching out a bronze arm he gave me the strength not to burst into tears. "*De l'audace, encore de l'audace....*" Slowly I walked down the subway steps. Henry, at the railing above the entrance, slowly disappeared from my sight.

All week long, as I was getting ready to move out of my room at Aline's I could only think of Henry. We would never make love again. And it was all my own doing. My self-respect demanded that I no longer see him, although I became a little more distraught each day. One radiant early summer morning I took the subway from Cité Universitaire to Le Plessis. I had to prepare the small apartment there, empty since 1949, for my family and myself. My joy at the forthcoming reunion with my parents had disappeared. It was putting an end to the happiest time in my life.

In Le Plessis the windows in every apartment of the housing development where we had lived for so many years were wide open. Once again snatches of Piaf's songs, played on the neighbors' radios, floated into the apartment. The apartment had the slightly threatening atmosphere of places where the past is still alive, preserved in the disarray of everyday objects that have been left untouched for a long time. I set out to break the spell, sweeping and scrubbing.

I shut our windows tightly. I hated Piaf, and I was about to hate my parents. I most certainly hated the apartment where, except for the war years, I had lived since my early childhood. Once again I would travel for hours in and out of Paris on subways and buses, and do the housekeeping in the tiny place overflowing with Russian books and papers. I would come home at fixed hours. I knew that my parents would assume that I'd live in Le Plessis as long as they themselves were in France.

My mother would do the shopping and cooking and set unexpected, lovely still lifes for me to draw. Sometimes she would sit down and draw with me—she herself was an excellent painter. For my part I would keep everything clean—I could not stand a messy house while my mother did not seem to notice dust or disorder. I would help Sasha with his homework, and he would try to teach me how to play chess.

I picked up the bunch of daisies that I had bought on my way from the subway. I could not resist them as I had passed the old familiar flower stand near the Métro: they had looked so bright, as if they were trying to comfort me. I put them in a white-and-gold pitcher I remembered from infancy and set them on the oval table in the dining room–kitchen. And suddenly all the happiness of my childhood years in Le Plessis was right there, in the kitchen with the redbrick floor, alive like the daisies shining against the old yellow-and-green-checkered oilcloth

"I must paint these," I thought to myself. All would be well; all I had to do was not to think about Henry. My father had said in a letter that he had written a new cycle of poems about Russia. He would read them aloud to us. We would go to the Louvre together and look at the Delacroix and at Courbet's *Studio*. Then the four of us would travel to the south of France where I had never been. I might fall in love with a Catalan fisherman, as handsome as Henry and a lot kinder.

But my mood changed when I left the apartment in Le Plessis. Walking to the subway through the park of my childhood, which, though now open to the public, was as sheltering and stately as ever, I made a discovery: I was missing Henry as I had never missed anyone before. I longed for him with the intensity with which I had longed for the mythical apache. To forget Henry would be very hard. I would miss the dinners, the conversations, and especially the old iron bed. This bed had become central to my life. How had I allowed this to happen? It was as if a second Olga was at my side, sharing in my affairs and giving me directions. It was intolerable, I was not ready to cohabit with this other woman, but I did not know what to do to drive her away.

I was back at Aline's just as an orange twilight was beginning to settle on Parc Montsouris. From the subway I took a shortcut through the park. I wondered how people in love who have no parks in which to relax and ponder their feelings can manage. As I came in, Aline, Olivier, and Jean-Pierre were drinking tea in the dining room of the apartment, which smelled of camphor. Aline's parents had just left for Brittany, and Aline and Olivier were about to go to the movies in the Latin Quarter. Jean-Pierre too was ready to leave, but instead the four of us lingered. Aline made another pot of tea and brought out some bread and jam. It was good to have the apartment to ourselves, to be drinking tea at dinnertime instead of sitting down to a routine, daily supper.

We watched the carpet formed by treetops of Montsouris turn black as the sky above reddened. Aline and Olivier tried to persuade me into coming to see Chaplin's *City Lights* with them, but I had seen it with Henry not long before. They left and I stayed back and chatted on with Jean-Pierre, who was in no hurry to go. The vigorous house-cleaning had tired me out. The oncoming darkness was soothing.

Jean-Pierre was a cheerful, tall man with a red beard. He never took off his French beret, even at dinner with Alice's parents or mine. Everyone was dismayed but forgiving—Jean-Pierre was so amusing, so earthy! He was a gifted natural painter. In my opinion, the old-fashioned academic instructions he was getting at the Beaux-Arts were not at all what he needed, but I was careful never to express my doubts. For Jean-Pierre to be enrolled at the Beaux-Arts was a triumph, it gave him self-esteem and social status. Without this he, the son of a postal worker in the thirteenth arrondissment, would never have been befriended by Olivier and Aline, the children of a celebrated academic family.

Jean-Pierre was describing his picture for the Prix de Rome competition. Like Olivier, he had recently been shut up in a *loge*, where he had painted an oil on the subject of the Furies pursuing Orestes. As I listened I thought of my mother, who was especially fond of Jean-Pierre. She used to be less self-restrained than I on the subject of the Beaux-Arts. "Jean-Pierre," she would say, "you are so lucky! You are an outdoor painter, a true French outdoor painter! Why don't you trade your beret for a straw hat and go into the sunshine to paint? Why do you let them shut you up in a dank studio?" My mother had a special liking for Jean-Pierre—she called him "Fénelon, l'educateur des jeunes filles," in memory of the French cleric who had authored *Traité De l'education des filles*: Jean-Pierre was so very protective of Alice and me.

I listened to Jean-Pierre, leaning back in the old-fashioned dining room chair with an upholstered leather back. Suddenly he said across the table, "Olga, when you lift your arms as you do now, I see a beautiful woman in you! Why don't you forget the ridiculous ideas you and Aline have inherited from the old maids at the lycée? Come to bed with me—or are you in love with that stiff American I met with you the other day? *Quelle catastrophe* that would be! I simply can't believe it!"

I said nothing, my arms stretched out above my head. Jean-Pierre got up and came around and slowly stroked the inside of my arms. "Let's go to Vaux-de-Cernay in the Rambouillet forest. No one will know we are there. We'll sketch the waterfalls and the beautiful rocks—Corot and Cézanne have painted them. There is so much I can teach you! I bet your good-looking American knows nothing of lovemaking." He was still caressing me.

With an effort I brought my arms down. I was tempted to accept Jean-Pierre's offer. Henry did not love me, and as a matter of fact, for years, I had wanted to see the Vaux-de-Cernay and the rocks once painted by Corot and Cézanne. Then I remembered that Jean-Pierre loved me even less than Henry. All he wanted to do was to be able to discuss me in private, man to man, with Olivier. I sat up straight. I wondered, what would my mother think now of the "educateur des jeunes filles"? I had reason to believe that her liberal ideas in matters of education were purely theoretical—I was careful not to put them to the test.

"You needn't worry, Jean-Pierre," I said, "my good-looking American is quite competent, although of course you at the Beaux-Arts are the experts. But perhaps instead of Vaux-de-Cernay you'd come with me to the Gare Saint-Lazare tomorrow at three? My parents will have lots of luggage."

Jean-Pierre did not look disappointed in the least. "Let me know if you change your mind, *ma vieille*," he said lightly. "For Olga and

Vadim"—my parents' first names—"I'll borrow my brother-in-law's *quatre-chevaux*."

I went to bed feeling better than I had all day. Jean-Pierre had momentarily diverted the disruptive Olga, the one who was obsessed with the creaky old bed at 31, rue de Seine.

CHAPTER NINE

Collioure

The four of us camped in a small round cove about a mile south of Collioure on the French coast of Catalonia. We settled our little tent and our cooking equipment right on the beach of hard packed gray sand. Above us large rocks interlaced with thyme and lavender sent drifts of fragrant air down to the water. It was sunny and hot day after day. My father and I swam for hours around the deep coves and the rocks, which edged the coast like delicate black embroidery while Sasha went for long explorations on his own and my mother read in the shade. The nights were so warm that we would sleep right on the beach outside our tent, only four or five feet from the still water.

We stayed on the beach for a whole month—it didn't rain once. In the late morning we would walk to the town of Collioure for coffee and sandwiches at civilized cafés, where the tables were shaded with striped parasols and sugar cubes were served in little paper wrappers. On our way to town just before noon we stopped at the open market held daily on the town's main square. Catalan peasants who barely spoke French sold vegetables and fruit there from wooden stalls shaded with canvas awnings.

They had come down on foot from their villages perched high above the sea. The small donkeys now resting in the shade of the square's plane trees had carried their rounded baskets of produce down narrow rock-strewn paths that meandered down the terraced mountainside. The old people, men and women, wore black and had sunburned faces of archaic nobility. In Collioure, time seemed to have stopped.

Each day we bought enormous tomatoes and freshly caught slithery sardines. For supper we grilled these on an open fire on the beach. I felt calmer than I had in Paris, but once in a while I had to think hard about Danton, betrayed by the Revolution and yet heroic to the end, to prevent myself from bursting into tears. I had said nothing to my parents about my love affair. To my knowledge neither had anyone else.

Day after day I tried not to think about Henry. In my mind, endlessly, I sketched pictures of Collioure as we saw it when we approached it in the noonday heat—the pink Moorish tower above the gentle curve of the harbor. But in fact, although I had brought a drawing pad and a bottle of india ink with me, I found it too hot on the beach to draw landscapes. All I could do in the shade of the rocks in the afternoons was read a little. I was slowly making my way through *The Beast in the Jungle*. Was Henry like John Marcher, who didn't even notice that poor May was in love with him? Where was Henry now?

I would paint Collioure as soon as we got back to Le Plessis— the three interlocking coves of the harbor, the Grecian-looking fishing boats beached on the sand, the pink watchtower Matisse had painted in his youth. Whenever I concentrated hardest on a future painting, Henry's face would float before my eyes and then disappear. It was uncanny. Here was Henry, smiling at me, as he had across the snowfield in the Jura. It was his happy face I saw, the one with the blue eyes that shone through only at times. Whenever I had this vision, I felt something akin to physical pain. It was all my fault. What did I care whether Henry met my parents or not? He was lost to me through my own obstinacy. A temporary cure was to go for a swim, alone, in the silky warm water.

Days went by with extraordinary rapidity. The wild oats that grew above the edge of the cove turned white and brittle. The smell of lavender became less strong. It was time to go back to Le Plessis. But the sea was so blue, so still, that we postponed our departure day after day. My mother, who had been brought up in Italy, was happy in Collioure. She quoted Colette, who had a house further north, in Saint Tropez: "The colors that rule here are those of dreams elsewhere—but, on the shore of Provence, these dreams are the reality."

Finally, one day at dawn, upon our arrival in Le Plessis after a night spent on the express train from Barcelona to Paris, which made a three-minute stop in Collioure, I found a postcard from Henry. It had the bell tower of Saint-Germain on one side. On the other, Henry had written in his most careful handwriting: "Dear Olga, How are you? I have decided that, so as to see you on occasion I'd meet the white whale itself, let alone your parents. I am away till September 10th, but after that please write to me. Gilkey and I would love to come to dinner in Le Plessis. Love, Henry."

I read the postcard time and again as I slowly walked up the stairs from the first-floor landing where the mailboxes were located in Le Plessis. From my yet unpacked rucksack I took out my best postcard from Collioure, the one with the pink Moorish watch-tower. I wrote to Henry at 31, rue de Seine, inviting him and Gilkey to dinner on the thirteenth of September, which was a Saturday.

The next morning, while unpacking our only encrusted jeans and faded bathing suits, I said to my mother as casually as I knew, "By the way, I am inviting two friends to dinner next Saturday. Two Americans. One is a poet. The other is working on a thesis about Mark Twain. I am sure I must have described Gilkey in my letters to you. We met on the *Liberté* last winter. He is very amusing, very talkative. I'll make the dinner if you like. What about eggplant caviar and beef with carrots? It will taste good after the picnic food in Collioure."

My mother said with her usual perspicacity, "Yes, I remember, you did write about the Mark Twain scholar who is so talkative. You said that aboard the *Liberté* he had courted our friend Anya. Is the other one then—the poet—a suitor of yours? What is he like?"

My mother was preoccupied with my "suitors"—she used the old-fashioned Russian term, *poklonniki*. She had an exaggerated sense of their number, a notion which she found worrisome. Like Aline, she detected a frivolous streak in me that alarmed her. I said in a detached voice, "Well, he is not exactly a suitor, he is a friend. He took me out to dinner in the Latin Quarter last winter. Vadim will like him, he is interested in literature. His name is Henry—Henry Carlisle. He grew up in San Francisco, but his family comes from

Nantucket Island in New England, from that small island described in *Moby-Dick*."

Early on Saturday morning I went shopping at the outdoor market, which was held twice a week along the main street of Le Plessis. It was hot. The market was overflowing with a late-summer harvest, the flower stand laden with dahlias and asters and big, harsh yellow daisies. Used to Paris's frequently cool summers, I savored this Indian summer. Gusts of happiness rolled over me like waves in the sea wind: I would see Henry again, visit him on rue de Seine.

I took a long time choosing the carrots and the eggplant from the greengrocer with the kindly eyes, a man who had looked one hundred years old for as long as we had lived in Le Plessis, with his wrinkled face and his fingers like sticks of gnarled wood. After buying the roast I looked for the right flowers, which would tell Henry that I had not forgotten the tulip season on rue de Seine.

"Mademoiselle, you must be crazy, you'd have to go to South America to find tulips in this season," said my longtime friend, the flower merchant, in a hurt voice. "Be sensible, take some roses." Instead, I bought an enormous bunch of orange dahlias and one of the blood red asters—they looked magnificent together. There were so many flowers that my mother looked startled when I came in. "I want to paint these," I said defensively. "Have you ever seen orange dahlias like these before?"

But the dahlias remained unpainted. I spent that whole day cooking and cleaning the apartment. My brother was away at my aunt Natasha's, and this made my task easy and the prospective dinner less risky—Sasha, like my mother, was extremely perceptive. At exactly seven-thirty when the doorbell rang, everything was ready, and I was beyond myself with nervousness. My father, vaguely aware of my state and anxious to help, went to open the door.

My parents were in their late forties then. They were both elegant and very shy. As adolescents they had been forced to leave their own civilized world, that of the progressive, prerevolutionary Russian intelligentsia for a forbidding new one—emigration. In France they had to learn to be poor and isolated, to be anonymous. Though they had met in Paris, both came from families that had been acquainted with each other before the revolution. They were remarkably well attuned to each other, one of the happier couples I have known.

By 1951, after two years in New York, where my father worked in the secretariat of the United Nations, my parents had encountered only a few Americans, and they were apprehensive at the prospect of meeting my new friends. Their American stay had coincided with McCarthy's most violent campaign against alleged Communists. To my parents, America was a country of intimidated citizens bullied by vociferous reactionaries. I argued with them, reminding them of my year at Bard College, and of their own friends on Long Island, the Huntingtons.

A Quaker family from Saint James, Long Island, the Huntingtons had, through the United Nations, invited my parents for a weekend at the shore. They had turned out to be well-read, generous, full of energy. They restored to some degree my parents' faith in America. Once my parents had joined the Huntingtons for a "working week end" held by Quakers in the slums of Long Island. My mother was very proud to have climbed on a ladder of vertiginous height to help paint a church steeple.

What with Gilkey's involvement with Mark Twain, whom Russians elevate to the rank of their own classics, and Henry's Nantucket Quaker background, I had been able to fairly reassure my parents, especially my father, about our guests. He was more open to the world than my mother, more self-assured, more curious about new people.

Tall, slender, and yet athletic, my father had graying wavy hair and the kind of ascetic, elongated face that is more often seen on Russian icons than in real life. He spoke French fluently but was a bit cavalier with French grammar. To him, only his native Russian, the language in which he wrote poetry, mattered. On the other hand, my mother spoke four languages excellently. She was small and delicate, with light brown hair untouched by gray. With her high cheekbones, she always had looked much younger than her age, and people often assumed that we were sisters. Routinely in the street she was addressed as "Mademoiselle."

I felt protective of my mother—she was often seized by extreme shyness, the result of her early years in France spent in the harsh world of couture. She and her twin sister, Aunt Natasha, had to work there as draftswomen for Jeanne Lanvin. My mother ascribed her inability to pursue fully her avocation as a painter to the accursed figurines that she and her sister had had to draw for years to earn money—the fashion sketches that, in her opinion, had weakened her artist's hand and eye. It took her years to return to painting, but even then she had always put my father's literary activities ahead of her own work.

The evening started effortlessly—Gilkey took over. Speaking profusely and rapidly, he recounted his solemn day at the Sorbonne. Before an awesome board of professors, which had included the celebrated Jean Wahl, he had successfully defended his thesis in French. Then my father told about his adventures at the Sorbonne: he had studied Russian linguistics there in the twenties, at a time when not a single Sorbonne professor of Russian spoke a word of the language.

I only half listened: the Henry who had come in was the one from Boissia, who had looked at me with smiling eyes across the snowy meadow in the Jura. Serving dinner helped me keep my composure. The five of us sat down at the oval dining room table covered with an old embroidered Russian tablecloth, one of the few things brought out of Russia by my grandmother during the Russian civil war. The eggplant caviar, spread on thin slices of black bread earned me a smile of recognition from Henry. With it my father poured out little glasses of ice cold vodka, though as a rule my parents seldom drank anything alcoholic.

I was given wings by the fact that Henry and my father were clearly liking each other. Henry was telling us about Nantucket, and about Melville, who had sailed around the South Sea Islands on one of his family's whalers. It was this voyage that had inspired *Typee*, a novel that my parents had read not long before. Everyone talked late into the evening about *Typee*. Henry said that it was an excellent, traditional nineteenth-century sea story. My parents saw philosophical depths in a novel that shows how relative and accidental our code of morals is.

"Your friend Henry is very attractive," my father said after the two left in time to catch the last Métro to Paris. He said this with a certain finality of tone meant to offset my mother's reactions, which were usually more guarded. "Please ask him to bring some of his poems next time. Perhaps you or your mother would translate them into Russian for me?"

CHAPTER TEN

Paris in the Fall

I went back to rue de Seine to find it even lovelier than in the springtime. Henry now worked for Fawcus. He was developing an all-consuming interest in publishing. The iron bed was right there to fall into whenever I visited. And, to my delight, during that first dinner in Le Plessis Henry had been charmed by my father. It was decided that we would soon have an evening of poetry together, a joint poetry reading. My mother and I would translate some of my father's poems into French for Henry while Henry would put one or two of his own into French for my parents.

Henry could see for himself that my parents did not wish me to marry—anyone. In fact, he found what he perceived as their dependence on me a little strange. At that time, in order to stay on in Paris, my parents who had never taken the French nationality because of my father's sense of Russianness, had to fulfill lengthy formalities at the Paris Préfecture, the police headquarters on Ile de la Cité. Since I was French by birth, I sometimes escorted my parents there and helped them with the awesome paperwork.

Henry and I had one or two conversations about Aline's contention that "my parents wanted to keep me for themselves." Henry would say, "In San Francisco, in my parents' milieu, people are born into a given generation and they stay within it. They spend little time with people younger or older than themselves. I guess your parents' attitude can be explained by émigré uncertainties. Unlike them, you are at home in France."

I disagreed. "I think that it has more to do with Russian traditions than with any sort of uncertainty. Remember *War and Peace*, how everyone in the Rostov family is involved with everyone else? I am dependent on my parents in the most fundamental way. No less than they on me. We give each other a reason to live. It's part of our tradition. My parents believe that one day the terror in Russia will end, that we'll be able to go live there. Not that I believe it myself. It has been too long—thirty years. The Bolsheviks will never give up their kingdom."

"What about your mother? She seems so helpless, somehow."

"My mother had a harrowing adolescence during the revolution. I hope she'll write about it some day, her story will read like something out of Dickens. It haunts her to this day. My father and I join forces whenever she is depressed, and we succeed in cheering her up. My mother is magnificent in times of crisis.

"One day I'll tell you our wartime adventures on the island of Oléron, the things she did while my father was arrested by the Germans for his work for the resistance. How she pacified the German officers who were ready to ransack our house on Oléron. Speaking to them in her cultured German, she convinced them not to break open an old armoire that, unbeknownst to us all, was full of hunting guns."

This story bewildered Henry. It was hard for him to imagine my mother as a heroine of the French resistance. Ignorant of the French rental customs, he could not quite understand why we had lived for five years with a closed armoire in our house. But he liked this wartime story, anyway.

There were no more arguments between us about my spending the night at 31, rue de Seine. Now, whenever I visited in the evening, Henry walked me to the Gare du Luxembourg willingly. Each time we would invent a new route from rue de Seine and discover new sights within the Latin Quarter.

From Danton's statue near the Odéon Métro we would walk up rue de Tournon, to the side entrance of the Luxembourg gardens, where the Fontaine de Médecis is nestled. Mossy and moist in the depths of the park, it looks like a baroque vision of the female sex, though the statuary around it, shimmering white in the darkness, gives it classic dignity. Then we would greet George Sand, who appears distracted, a lady in a very ample skirt stranded in the middle of an oval flower bed.

Or else from place de l'Odéon we followed rue Monsieur le Prince. It had been named for le Grand Condé, a flamboyant seventeenth-century prince who had been a famous general. Where did his palace stand, we wondered, had his guard lived nearby? We peered at the restaurants along that street—an Italian one, a Chinese one, all red lacquer and gold. I had never been to a Chinese restaurant—it looked tantalizing beyond its half-drawn lace curtains. Henry told me about Shanghai, where he had been with the navy during the war. I was shocked by his stories about beautiful Russian émigré girls there, who had to work as prostitutes in order to survive. Henry maintained that they were not really that. He tried to explain the difference between B girls and prostitutes. B girls are paid to entice night club customers to buy more drinks.

One day in October, a couple of weeks before classes started at the Sorbonne, Henry invited me to meet him in a café on rue Soufflot near the Panthéon. The Panthéon was a monument that especially pleased Henry. As we passed it he would remind me that the Surrealists had advocated that it be sawed in half, each half set a meter apart, just for the hell of it, he said. And when we admired Notre Dame, Henry took pleasure in telling me that Cocteau had decreed that it really looked like a pair of oversized binoculars standing on end.

On that drizzly evening, Henry was going to have dinner with Fawcus, while I was at Aline's, but before that, at dusk, we were to have a drink together. The days were growing short. As I came out of the Métro on place du Luxembourg the city was already gray. The evening lights glistened, a faint smell of fallen leaves floated from the Luxembourg gardens. It was time to plan for the next school year. I thought back to my room at Aline's. I had been so free there and the spring so lengthy and delectable. I had been back from America for less than a year, but it seemed like a lifetime. A lifetime of happiness.

The café chosen by Henry was more luxurious than our usual meeting places. It had benches upholstered in red velvet and gilded columns framing a multitude of mirrors. At first I could not find Henry in the midst of all the glitter. Finally I spotted him at the back of the café. As he looked at me across the large room, he had the smiling eyes from Boissia. He ordered us two glasses of mulled wine and said, "Olga, I have something very important to tell you, but please excuse me first," and he disappeared into the men's room.

When Henry returned he sat down again somewhat stiffly. He swallowed a little wine. Then he took my hand across the table and said solemnly, "Olga, I love you. Will you marry me?" I settled back on the velvet seat and closed my eyes, keeping Henry's hand in mine.

"Yes," I said.

"An English aunt has left me a small inheritance," Henry said. "I can keep you in style for a couple of years while I finish my studies. You too can study whatever you want. Let's get married soon." I had no idea that the thought of living with Henry would make me as happy as it did. But that he loved me made me even happier. I leaned forward across the table and we kissed for a long time.

When Henry had gone off to his dinner I ordered another glass of hot wine. I stayed on in the glittering café, happiness rolling over me like waves that follow each other on the beach without quite catching up with each other.

After a while I went downstairs to telephone Aline, but it was Olivier who answered. I said that something unexpected had happened, that I could not be there for dinner. Would he apologize to his mother and tell Aline that I'd call her the next day? He said he would, then added, "Jean-Pierre is coming to dinner, he will be disappointed not to see you. You never come by anymore—don't tell me that you still go out with that American!"

"As a matter of fact I do," I said quickly, and hung up.

I went back to my half-empty glass of wine, now cool, and anxiety came over me. I could not understand it at first—why this icy feeling? Surely not because of Olivier's remark. I was happy, almost as happy as on that day at the end of the war when the Germans had released my father from prison. I would spend the rest of my life with Henry. He would write poems and perhaps work in publishing, and I would paint and keep house. We would buy a large bed and sleep in it together every night. Together we would travel to Nantucket and to the south of France.

Then I knew that what I was dreading was my parents' reaction to Henry's proposal, or rather, to my acceptance of it. I had kept the thought away for as long as I could, but now I had to face it. My wine was cold, I could not stay forever in this café. I had to go back to Le Plessis and tell them—immediately. Otherwise my happiness would fade away.

Part of me agreed with the arguments my parents were certain to put forth. There was willfulness in my wanting to marry Henry. I was young, and I had no profession yet. Henry and I came from different parts of the world, with only a fragile bridge between us made of a few poems and books. Henry was a patriotic American, whereas my father viewed America as the oppressor of the working people, and a particular enemy of everything that was Russian. I struggled with an absurd notion, to be sure, that Henry, an intelligent, honest man, would alter someday—but when? I would have to leave behind whatever stability Paris and my French friends had given me. Become an émigré all over again in America. My search for the immediate had brought me to a point where I had to choose a future.

As for Henry, although he had said nothing about it, surely in proposing to me he was going against all that was expected of him back in San Francisco. What would his parents say to his marrying the descendant of a family of revolutionaries, banned from Russia even before the revolution for their connection with secret terrorist organizations? To his marrying someone without money, who wanted to become a painter, and, generally speaking, lead a life of high romance?

It was unclear to me why Henry would want to marry me, except that he was in love, a fact that he had, consciously or not, kept from me, not withstanding that postcard he had sent at the end of the summer and which I knew by heart: ". . . so as to see you on occasion I'd meet with the white whale itself." I had assumed all along that though enamored, Henry did not wish to regard our love affair as anything permanent.

My parents had finished dinner when I came home—my brother had already gone to bed. "Is everything all right?" my mother asked. Then she said, "Whatever the reasons that bring you home, it is wonderful to have you back early for once. We may finish reading aloud that last chapter of the Berdyaev autobiography, which we'll have to give back to the library next week. And look, we have this wonderful plum tart made by your aunt Natasha—let's have a cup of tea with it."

I poured tea for the three of us and sat down at the oval dining table. My mother was getting up to look for the Berdyaev volume when I spoke up in a voice that quivered a little: "Please stay right there. I want to tell you something important. Henry Carlisle has asked me to marry him and I said yes. We are in love. We will be married soon." I glanced at my parents. They looked stunned.

No one said anything for what seemed like a very long time. Then to my relief my father spoke first. "Olga, I will not make you unhappy by trying to get you to change your mind, and it would be useless in any case. Let's instead look reasonably at your unreasonable idea. For it is that—unreasonable, not to say foolish. Why should you want to get married now? Why not stay with us for a year or two longer? You know so little about the world! You have just begun your studies! However, I do want you to know that I like Henry very much. He strikes me as a man of honor. He is handsome. I like the fact that he is committed to literature—you'll have that in common for as long as you are together."

My mother said nothing. She looked sad. I felt sorry for her and came around behind her and embraced her. She said, "All we want is for you to be happy. When do you want to get married?"

"Before you go back to America—what do you think, would that be convenient?" My father's words had lifted an enormous weight off my soul. In due time my mother would come to share his view.

Later that evening I was falling asleep when my mother came into my room. I switched on my small reading light and then turned it off again as my mother sat down on the edge of the bed. She said intently, "You can't be serious, Olga! You can't get married! To someone you barely know! Please wait. Come back with us to New York, get a degree from Columbia. Your father is brave, but I know that, for him, to have you marry a man whose country might go to war against Russia at any moment is devastating."

I said hotly, "That's not true, he does not think like that! The fact that Henry is a writer is what matters to him. Please, don't be upset. And think, you'll never have to worry about my suitors again!" My mother sighed, she gave me a hug in the dark and left.

My mother was never to say anything more against my marrying Henry. In fact, she never said anything critical of Henry for as long as she lived. Henry, however, remained secretly wary of her. Many years later he reported that once, shortly before our wedding, in a last effort to undo our engagement, my mother had asked him how he planned to deal with the suitors that, according to her, appeared wherever I went. Henry had found the question provocative; he had been shocked. But then perhaps there had been a misunderstanding? My mother's English was not perfect in those years.

CHAPTER ELEVEN

Wedding in Le Plessis

The day after he proposed, Henry sent a letter to his parents announcing his engagement to a young Parisian of Russian parentage. Henry worked hard on this letter, a model of epistolary eloquence that the Carlisles preserved and proudly showed to me years later. The Carlisles replied with an affectionate telegram inviting us to come to Nantucket the following summer. I was also told that Lita Ilyn, "the Russian lady who had the most perfect manners of anyone in the world," had played a part in this turn of events.

When he received Henry's letter about his plans to marry a Miss Andreyev, Henry's father, Henry Senior, telephoned Mrs. Ilyn. Did she know anything about the Andreyevs? he asked. Though Mrs. Ilyn was a White Russian, a monarchist who regarded both my father's and my mother's Socialist families with dismay for their role in helping to bring down the Russian Empire in 1917, she was nonetheless able to reassure the Carlisles. Lita Ilyn, who was to become a very close friend of mine decades later, knew Leonid Andreyev's writings. She did not mention his revolutionary views, she only said that I came from a well-known Russian literary family. Though not at all aristocratic, my family was socially acceptable. The Carlisles admired Mrs. Ilyn. From that moment on they decided that a well brought up young woman from a respectable family could only be a good addition to their daughterless family. All the more, since Henry caused his parents concern because of his taste for life abroad and his refusal to embrace a serious profession such as his father's—Henry Carlisle Senior was a well-regarded, successful mining engineer in San Francisco.

One afternoon in late November I went to the Mairie of Le Plessis to fill out the documents necessary for my marriage to Henry. Our Mairie, or town hall, was housed in the stylish, rundown eighteenth-century manor house that stood at the edge of that park that had been so much a part of my childhood. That day in late fall the shapes of the trees were visible through the last leaves. After a rainy night the park smelled of mushrooms.

As I came out onto the terrace that stretched before the Mairie, I turned around to look at the wide view of the meadow, now a soccer field, and of the park beyond it, each tree on the horizon like a head of curly blond hair aflame against the blue black sky. Suddenly I was seized with doubts. What if my parents were right and I should not marry yet and wait a year or two? Go back to America with them? I sat down on the low stone wall that enclosed the terrace. Everything around me was very still.

After some minutes I went into the Mairie. In the drafty office established in what once must have been the vestibule of the manor, I filled out a stack of legal papers. Then I went out again onto the terrace, hoping for some sign telling me whether I was making the right decision, but all was silent except for a faint church bell somewhere in the distance. The weather was turning cold, the sky had darkened, the curly heads of the trees on the horizon were no longer burning.

The next day, my father took me for a walk in the park. We looked for mushrooms as we walked along the leaf-strewn alleys. On our way home, my father said, "Olga, as a small child, even before you knew how to read and write, you composed poems. Your mother and I always felt that we were the custodians of someone gifted. Now that you are marrying, you'll have to take care of that person yourself. Before the war, your uncle Daniel in Moscow, to whom we sent some of your childhood drawings, wrote that you would one day uphold the Andreyev artistic legacy. You have that responsibility, you cannot expect Henry to do that for you. Henry is a writer, he has his own talent to nurture. Of course, as long as we live we'll help you, but essentially you will be on your own."

I had never heard my father speak as confidently about whatever gifts I might have. I was surprised and touched. I said, "Certainly

Henry would never interfere with my decision to become a painter. For my part I'll try to help him with the literary work he will pursue. As for painting, I know that it is up to me, alone."

I was thinking of my mother, who in her youth had all but stopped painting for the sake of a harmonious family life. Was my father aware of it? Only in midlife was my father to encourage her to pick up her brushes again. As for Henry, he was critical by nature. I could not expect enthusiastic endorsements from him, only good-humored support, and that was more than any other young man I had met had offered me. The notion that we might have children was vague in my mind. All I knew was that I wanted very much to be a good wife to Henry. I could no longer imagine life without him. Nor did I want to know whether this was solely the wish of that other, disruptive Olga who thought so often about the creaky iron bed on rue de Seine. I was one with her.

My wedding to Henry was plain and cheerful.

Only my immediate Russian family was invited, and Aline. Remembering Henry's reaction to Olivier and Jean-Pierre, I did not ask any other French friend, with the exception of Cécile Grand-jouan, a Larcouëst friend of my parents' generation. Vic Breeden of San Francisco, who had played a diverting and sometimes disruptive role in Henry's childhood was his witness. Vic had turned up in Le Plessis unexpectedly, and he borrowed thirty dollars and a gray suit from Henry, neither of which he returned. (He made up for this by giving us a white Steinway baby grand piano for our twenty-fifth wedding anniversary.)

The wedding took place a few days before Christmas 1951, in the eighteenth-century manor house in Le Plessis by a Communist woman mayor. Her forceful presence did not strike Henry as a particularly good omen, but I quite liked her. The mayor was an articulate, bright-eyed woman of forty, fat and yet dignified in her dark suit belted with a wide tricolor ribbon, the symbol of her authority. She wished us happiness and many children and concluded the ceremony in less than five minutes.

PART II

In Henry's Country

CHAPTER TWELVE

The Attic

The house on Nantucket's Main Street was handsome and austere, untouched by the passage of time. The granite sills, pale gray against the brick facade, the stately entrance hall opening on four spacious parlors, the sparse yet elegant furniture, some of it chosen by the builder of the house himself—Henry Coffin, Henry's great-grandfather.

The house had been built in 1834, when Henry Coffin, a Quaker whaling merchant in partnership with his brother Charles, was sending vessels to the four corners of the world. When whaling declined in the middle of the nineteenth century, there was no money to renovate Nantucket. Like most of those in the town, Henry Coffin's house was unchanged for more than one hundred years. I had been eager to see it. I had fallen in love with America—with a literary version of America. Isabel Archer and Ishmael were at the heart of my new life.

When I saw the island from the air for the first time, flying in from New York early one day in the spring of 1954, it had looked ethereal, a luminous crescent afloat on the pale blue-green Atlantic. But the bounce of the plane as we landed had been hard, and now the granite steps to the front door of 75 Main Street looked intimidating.

The light on that April afternoon was turning golden when we walked inside. The portraits of my husband Henry's ancestors observed me, the newest bride, with benevolent detachment. Henry

Coffin, the master of the house, dark haired, blue-eyed, substantial looking, was settled against a rosy sunset, his cheeks rosy with good health, a picture of Victorian repose and respectability. His father-in-law, Levi Starbuck, leaned on his whalebone-handled walking stick, a shrewd, self-possessed merchant. Henry Coffin's daughter, Susan, sat under a tree in a pink dress, a moody ten-year-old with her father's elongated face and serious air. Eliza Starbuck Coffin, her mother, peered from under a lace bonnet. Her eyes were full of anxiety. Henry said that she had been read out of the Quaker meetinghouse for putting up a small stone marker on her father Levi's grave, a mark of ostentation unacceptable to the Society of Friends. Or was it the imminent demise of whaling and with it a secure and prosperous way of life that made her look so distraught?

A small back room with its bright redbrick fireplace had been used by the Coffins as both a family room and a home office. Here ships' captains came to discuss business matters with their employers, using the stairs going down to the garden. Some of Henry Coffin's own furniture was still there—a tall, many-compartmented desk where whaling records and bills were kept, a black horsehair rocking chair. We sat there for a while on spindly straight chairs. More vividly than any other in the house, this room evoked its former occupants. It was as if Henry Coffin had just stepped outside to take the air under the great pear trees, now gnarled and yet alive, which he had planted himself more than one hundred years before.

The sharing of property among Henry Coffin's children had left little furniture in the house. The bedrooms on the second floor were cold and bare, but the attic above, built of dark cedar, like an inverted ship's hull, was warm. It was a wide, beautifully proportioned space filled with a spicy fragrance of dry wood. In the half darkness, we made out harpoons and oars and scales. The attic was a mysterious-looking, chaotic repository of objects from Nantucket's whaling days, just as Henry remembered it from his childhood visits to the island.

From the unlit attic, a steep wooden ladder led us into a sun-warmed cupola that, like a bird's nest, overlooked the sharply pitched slate roof of the house. From there much of the island could be seen, surrounded by glistening waters the color of the sky. An orange sun was setting beyond Madeket, the inlet where the first settlers of the island—including Henry Coffin's ancestor, Tristram Coffin—had landed almost three hundred years before. The town— gray roofs, pink brick walls, and green branches touched with red by the sun—lay serenely below us. Standing there high above Nantucket I had a sense of well-being.

We could not stay in 75 Main Street that night: long shut up, it was now being restored as a summer house by Henry's father, who had inherited it some months before, at the death of his sister Elsie. It was dark outside when we locked the front door with a massive brass key and set out in search of the boarding house where we had reserved a room for the night.

Lower Main Street, with wooden and stone hitching posts still standing along its sidewalk, was deserted. The ghost of Nantucket's most celebrated visitor, Ishmael, seemed about to step forth, looking for Queequog and the Try Pot Inn. We found our rooming house on Center Street and settled in. Since it had no dining room we soon went out again, to Cy's Green Coffee Pot, the one restaurant open off-season on Nantucket in those days. We were hungry, and the clam chowder there proved worthy. "Remember *Moby-Dick*," Henry said, "how Ishmael and Queequog lived on chowder—clam chowder or cod chowder, or both, day after day, as they waited for the *Pequod* to sail?"

Then he told me about his visits to the island as a child, coming by train and ferry from California, when 75 Main Street belonged to his Aunt Elsie, a spinster imbued with reverence for her Coffin background. "When I knew her, she was very much the mistress of Nantucket despite her age and poverty—she drove around the island in a regal old Hudson," said Henry. "She took me to the island's wild beaches to watch the waves crash against the shore. She was the first to point out to me that the sea had a song of its own, which one could listen to for hours. We agreed that there were two things one could watch forever: the surf and flames in the hearth." They did both together in silence.

After dinner we went out again to explore Nantucket's wharves, which appeared abandoned in those years, with only a few dim lights reflected in the black waters of the harbor. We strolled along Old North Wharf, which had once belonged to the Coffins. The ghostly pier was lined with small gray boathouses used in the summer as vacation cottages, now boarded up. The "Charles and Henry," the "Constitution," the "Lydia," the carved wooden nameboards proclaimed—the very same boards that had identified the sturdy whaling ships on their journeys around the globe.

Then we walked up Main Street and studied Henry Coffin's house in the moonlight, and the almost identical one that his brother Charles had built across the street. The night was clear and cold. The twin houses with their shuttered windows looked like outsized seashells, tightly closed upon themselves. Holding hands, we stared at 75 Main Street in silence. I found it handsome and yet, standing there on the sidewalk I felt very much an outsider. I sensed that Henry did, too. He was far away from California.

In the days that followed, we spent hours in the attic of Henry Coffin's house. There were endless treasures there. We looked at old maps, opened trunks filled with beautiful old clothes and chests overflowing with letters and diaries. We were handling objects that Captain Ahab would have used—a sextant, a compass, a logbook. We found a collection of African baskets, several boxes of mysterious-looking amulets wrapped in faded ribbons. The attic was a place where one wanted to stay forever; its cedar smell was addictive.

As we looked through the trunks and sea chests, Henry told me that there was something he especially wanted to find in the attic. Once, when he was eleven, Aunt Elsie had led him there. She had taken a wizened small thing wrapped in tissue paper out of a chest. It was a mummy's hand brought back from Egypt in the old days. It gave its owner the power of divination. But much as he looked, Henry was never able to recover Aunt Elsie's talisman. Had she given it away, or buried it in the garden? She would *not* have thrown it out, Henry insisted.

Russians are said by tradition to be besieged by inner doubts: I pondered the secrets beneath the orderly surface of the Coffins' lives. Was the Quakers' Peaceable Kingdom challenged by the necessities of business—the sight of harpoons and hooks and axes was ominous. Love of seafaring was coupled with a reverence for the home, touchingly expressed by samplers embroidered by small Coffin girls in the early part of the nineteenth century. A taste for exotic islands would have been obscured by a deliberate rejection of worldly pleasures. I thought back to our conversation about *Typee* the year before. On that first visit, the Russian in me had hoped that an answer to my search for the soul of America, for that of my husband, could be found in that fabulous attic. But my other self, the lighthearted Parisian, was repelled. I wanted an open, carefree existence—and France, which I had left for good, stood in my mind for such an existence.

CHAPTER THIRTEEN

Gramercy Park

W e had not been able to get to Nantucket for quite a while after our marriage. I became pregnant right away; many among our acquaintances assumed that we had married because of my pregnancy. Possibly Henry's parents did. They had invited us to the island as newlyweds. In their letters they expressed disappointment as we stayed on in Paris for another year. Evidently they feared that Henry might become an expatriate. They wanted him home with his new family, earning his living. Much as I loved Paris, I agreed with them. I did not want our son to belong to yet another generation of expatriates.

Michael's arrival had delayed my acquaintanceship with the senior Carlisles. In the fall of 1952 in Paris he was born promptly and painlessly at the plush American Hospital in Neuilly. Michael was three months old when we brought him to the United States. First, Henry took a graduate degree at Stanford University, then we settled in New York, where my parents had returned from Paris after the United Nations General Assembly. In a matter of a few weeks Henry found a job. He was hired as a junior editor by Alfred Knopf, which put him at the center of the publishing world of that era. Henry began editing history books for Alfred and in the words of Bill Koshlaud, one of his mentors at Knopf, the "exotic language books" for his wife, Blanche. These were principally French books, at a time when Camus and Sartre, acquaintances of hers, were first published in America. The Knopfs were the most charismatic, discerning literary publishers in New York. Both were eccentrics, unpredictable, but thanks to them, Henry received a first-rate education in publishing. They had been first to bring out Leonid Andreyev in the twenties, and they treated us both with the utmost cordiality.

My parents expected me to continue my studies and were determined to be of help. I applied to Hunter College. Miraculously, despite my skimpy Bard and Sorbonne records, I was admitted as a graduate student into the Fine Arts Department there. I majored in painting. In the evenings I rode the subway or the bus to school. Whenever I had some serious studying to do or a paper to write, my parents took charge of Michael. As a result, somewhat to Henry's concern, there was a brief period when Michael's Russian was more fluent than his English. Later on, with my parents' help, I would teach him how to read and write Russian. French came later, on a visit to Aline Pagès in Paris.

Michael was almost two when, on a second visit to Nantucket, we took him with us. I was eager to see the island again after our brief first visit there. Then, as I had looked in the faces of my husband's Quaker relations, I thought I had come close to having an insight into his secret self. Now, two years later, though Henry appeared to love me, and though I was as infatuated with him as ever—all the more for his reserve—we did not have the kind of day-to-day intimacy that my parents for instance shared, or his, for that matter. I both liked my independence and resented it. Married life forced me to make many decisions on my own while being accountable to someone else—my husband.

Henry liked to be by himself a good deal of the time. Sensing this, I drew back. It was easier to learn restraint than to appear overbearing, an invasive Russian. In fact, I too was weary of familial confrontations. There had been too many in my childhood during the war, when we all had lived under one roof with my grandmother and my aunts, a Russian clan given to emotional outbursts.

To my surprise, I quickly had gotten used to Michael's being, for all practical purposes, an unpredictable, astonishingly playful extension of myself, whether he was twisting in my arms, or jumping up and down in his stroller, or straining on my hand to break away and dash off across the street in search of adventure.

Misha, as he was called then, was extroverted and warmhearted.

With every month he was becoming better company. When I had first discovered that I was pregnant I was upset—somehow I could not imagine that it could have happened so quickly. At that time my mother had said, "Just think, you'll have a close friend—for the rest of your life." Now everything was happening faster than I expected, especially the necessity to face a whole array of new responsibilities. Caring for Michael came first, then there was Henry, his career in publishing, his parents, and finally my painting and my studies.

I tried to be rational about my various obligations. In this my training at the French lycée was crucial. Difficulties were to be formulated, analyzed, and then remedied as best one could. On one's own if at all possible. Instinctively I avoided discussing Henry with my parents. How could I explain to them, for instance, that while he often spoke to me of the rigidity of his own upbringing, he nonetheless felt that I was not disciplining Michael properly, that I was not firm enough, that my parents also spoiled him? A product of French education, I was in fact relatively strict in daily life—if anything, perhaps a little too much so: a desire to have everyday life run smoothly sometimes obscured my imagination.

Uncannily, Michael sensed whenever there was unspoken dissension between his parents on matters of discipline. He took delight in testing how far he could go before an open conflict would flare up. We discovered that we had given birth to a pint-size Machiavelli. However, by the age of three or four Michael realized that conflicts between his parents were not in his own best interest, and he ceased to indulge his divisive instincts. His exuberance simmered down a little. At five he had become a reasonably well-behaved little boy. As my mother had predicted, we became close friends.

Thanks to Henry's willingness to stay with Michael when he was not at work, I had a few hours each week in which to explore New York. Whenever I went to the Metropolitan Museum I was reminded of my daily visits to the Louvre only a couple of years before. Now I was enamored of the Met's *Venus with a Young Musician* by Titian. I would sit for hours in one of the halls painted a greenish blue, facing Cézanne's *Montagne Sainte-Victoire* and Van Gogh's *L'Arlésienne*.

I remember looking at the backlit woman with the sharp elbows, the darkened face. The burning yellow background behind her was what I was searching for, the light that would guide an aspiring artist. In New York the light was usually flat, a painter's despair. Sitting there in front of *L'Arlésienne*, for the first time in my life I felt exiled. I kept dreaming about Arles, where Van Gogh, a man from Northern Holland, had painted this willful looking woman against a yellow wall. I tried to recreate in my mind the pink watchtower at Collioure and the fluffy clouds above the Parc Montsouris.

Sometimes I went to the Met to study. For Robert Motherwell, my teacher at Hunter, I was working on a paper about Whistler, the artist who had challenged the Victorian conventions of his day with such impertinent brilliance. Though there were no Whistlers shown there at the time, the Met was a good place to write. The museum was quite empty; emptier still was the formal but welcoming Frick Gallery nearby, which had several Whistlers on display, including an elegant portrait of Montesquiou, one of the prototypes of Proust's Mr. de Charlus.

On mild days on weekends my brother, Sasha, and I took walks all over the city. Once, during our first New York spring, we came across something that seemed almost impossible to find even in those years—a small rent-controlled apartment for rent on Gramercy Park. Two rooms with a view of the park in an old brownstone.

A black janitor had beckoned us as we strolled around the park's tall iron grille. A flat was for rent from a Miss Thurlow, on the third floor of 10 Gramercy Park. We rang Miss Thurlow's bell: she lived on the main floor of the building. A middle-aged woman wrapped in dark veils, wearing a hat like Giraudoux's *Folle de Chaillot*, she agreed immediately to rent us the apartment available upstairs. Clearly she had liked my brother's youthful good looks. She was a painter from Philadelphia, a graduate of the academy there who proved a somewhat erratic yet well-meaning landlady for years to come. She willingly settled for Henry's good looks when she discovered that I was married to him and not to Sasha.

Our apartment at 10 Gramercy Park was very pretty, with a marble fireplace and an ample view of park greenery. Summer or winter, Michael and I spent hours inside Gramercy Park, a diminutive park to which we were granted a key. It was enclosed by a tall, spiky wrought iron grille and locked gates. A bronze statue of the Shakespearean actor Edwin Booth stood in its center. While Michael played I sketched trees or read Proust or Henry James's novels. They still were much needed "textbooks" in the art of self-restraint. I read and reread *The Wings of the Dove*. There, secret greed plays out in a city of masks, which I dreamed of visiting one day. *Washington Square*, with its setting similar to ours on Gramercy Park, was no less absorbing, about a New York that, I assumed, still existed somewhere nearby.

But the city, enormous, noisy, unpredictable, churned around the park where we were locked up for our safety. Walking out, pushing Michael's stroller on my way to the supermarket on Twenty-third Street and Lexington Avenue, I looked at the passersby, their faces intensely alive—black men, old women, beautiful girls, executives in gray flannel suits, derelicts. This was a harsh, exuberant city that might become mine one day. A forbidden volume of Henry Miller's *Tropic of Capricorn*, which we had brought with us from Paris, had given me a yearning for the vast, unruly metropolis beyond Gramercy Park.

In those first years, Michael and I spent a lot of time with my parents—they lived near Columbia University, which Sasha would soon be attending. We did what we had always done whenever we were together. In the evenings, we read Russian poetry aloud. Painterly Pasternak who had so often celebrated the glory of painting remained my beloved contemporary Russian poet—his father, his first wife had been painters. The audacity of his images, the roaring of his lines were a promise of liberation: no country that produced poets as free could be enslaved forever.

From our enclave in New York City, the fate of Tsvetayeva, who had been an intimate of my grandmother's until 1939, when she followed her husband to the USSR, was unknown to us as were those of my uncle Daniel and of Isaac Babel. We did not know if these people were alive, where they lived, whether they were still writing—riddles that would not be answered for years.

Passionately we followed the political events of the day. Stalin's death in 1953 proved to be a prodigious divide in our lives. I will never forget the moist, early spring morning when we heard the funeral music that announced his death over the radio. The air in

Gramercy Park was fragrant, with a trace of sea smell to it. It was a New York spring day that would also be a turning point for the whole world. My parents were overjoyed: though my father wanted to believe that socialism was an appropriate social system for Russia, what was known of Stalin had always filled him with loathing.

CHAPTER FOURTEEN

A Studio on Nantucket

S een from the air in good weather Nantucket looks like a fragment of sky drifting across the ocean. But as the plane lands abruptly on this azure fragment one becomes aware of the island's unrelieved flatness, of the low horizon enclosed by scrubby pine woods. The airy island is no more, the pull of gravity is overpowering.

I remember how huge the sky had looked on that hot August day in 1954, and the sweetness of the air after that of New York. Two figures were waving to us as we stepped out of the plane. They were Henry's parents, Henry and Mary Carlisle whom we had not seen in several months. There were greetings and hugs and Michael was passed around and squeezed and admired. He was an affectionate child whom the Carlisles described with satisfaction as "truly outgoing."

We took a drive on our way to 75 Main Street in Henry Senior's "yellow car," a stately old Ford convertible, which sailed majestically past the ancient windmill that stands guard at the edge of the town, and the cemetery where Henry's Quaker ancestors are buried in unmarked graves. Here were the silvery shingled houses, like grayhaired ladies in pearls behind their white picket fences, and the towering elms on Main Street that cast lacy shadows on the smooth, rounded cobblestones.

The town was as I remembered it from our first visit, a pristine vision of the American past, but now Henry Coffin's house hummed with what the Carlisles called "projects." In the back parlor we discussed these over drinks—a "sundowner," as Henry's parents called this ritual. Michael was taken to the old barn beyond the house, which had just been turned into a guest house. He went off readily with the teenage girl from the neighborhood who had been hired to take care of him during our vacation. Susan was plump and energetic and promised to be a good playmate. At two, Michael's eagerness for new friendships and new activities was boundless.

The back parlor—the old Coffin family room—had been transformed since Henry and I had last sat there. It no longer felt as if Henry Coffin was about to walk in silently through the garden door. His desk with the many rows of cubby holes had been moved to a place of honor in a front parlor. In addition to his black horsehair rocking chair there was now a plump upholstered sofa in the back parlor. Henry Senior, as I called him, said that it would soon become the "map room." He himself was framing some of the antique maps that had been found in the attic; these would be hung around the parlor's walls.

He unfolded some of these maps for us. Going back to the eighteenth century, they presented a wonderfully odd view of the world—a Florida as big as all of Africa on one, on another a Muscovy that lay directly next to Peking. Now Henry Senior was making us a round of cocktails. The ice tinkled, a soft sound that was convivial though it would have surely startled the teetotaling early inhabitants of 75 Main Street. So would the lighthearted conversation about the improvements undertaken around the house.

The Carlisles were engrossed in the work in progress—the turning of the old Coffin horse barn into what was now known as "the Barn"; a new kitchen at 75 Main Street, which Henry Senior, a mining engineer, had had ingeniously carved out of two closets; the whaling ledgers, which he was putting in chronological order. Then my parents-in-law praised their grandson: "Here is a fellow who truly loves people," Henry Senior said with pride. "Like his mother," he added with a friendly pat on my hand.

Across the room I saw Henry stiffen in Henry Coffin's rocking chair. I too stiffened. Henry's name was not mentioned, but it was about his alleged lack of sociability and his excessive love of books, which caused his parents a grief they did not try to hide. Henry's parents were distressed by their son's intellectual pursuits. His sense of independence was perceived as a flaw violating one of their fundamental convictions—that happiness and worldly success are the reward of those who possess the good-humored gregariousness practiced in earnest by my father-in-law: Henry Senior was proud of his having sent out more than three hundred Christmas cards every year.

But this was a lovely summer afternoon, and no one wanted to spoil this particular family reunion. My father-in-law dispelled the gathering clouds with a remark about his father-in-law, Captain Miles Gorgas. Everyone who had known him agreed that, although the captain was extremely well-read and spoke several languages, he had also been supremely outgoing, without peer—humorous, convivial, sharp-tongued yet good-natured, a legend to this day in San Francisco, where he had spent the last years of his life.

Henry, Jr., had been six when the captain died, but there had been time for a friendship between the two to develop. His grandfather's presence had been crucial to Henry: his parents had been too busy with their own pursuits—social for his mother, professional for his father—to be able to spend much time with him when he was small. But Captain Gorgas had taken him on walks, he had conversed with him as with an adult. Judging by his letters, carefully preserved by his daughter, my mother-in-law, Henry's literary gifts may have owed something to his grandfather, the captain. On the other hand, Henry's Coffin ancestors had had a dry, pragmatic approach to language and to their daily life. One could guess that the slaughter of whales as the source of their wealth did not excite or please them. Rather it was a grim necessity.

Prompted by her adoring husband, Mary Carlisle agreed to tell us one of Captain Gorgas's stories. She was fiftyish then and still very pretty. Her features were sharply drawn, she had a delicate profile. As a child she must have looked like Lewis Carroll's Alice. She still had a little of Alice in her—an essence of girlishness that had never gone away.

Mary chose an American story in my honor. A nice old-fashioned one about friendly, hard-drinking midshipmen fraternizing—Joseph McCarthy, though discredited by the recent army hearings, was still feared in America. In any case my parents-in-law were careful never to hurt my feelings as a Russian: politics were not discussed between us. I had heard Henry Senior say that, though his manner was objectionable, Senator McCarthy must have had some well-founded, patriotic reason to act as he did, and this in his mind made him a tolerable presence on the American political stage.

The astounding fact was that I had gotten used to this state of affairs. Only two years before, had I been told that I would become a member of a family that avoided mentioning politics, one that raised no objections to Senator McCarthy's political methods, I would not have believed it. But now I was listening to Mary's story with a pleasure only slightly touched by weariness as she told about the warm, rollicking friendships between American and Russian officers in Alaska at the turn of the century.

There was a surprise after dinner. As we were getting up to leave, Henry Senior, beaming with pleasure, announced that, in secret, he had created a studio in the Barn on Liberty Street. A painting studio. What with young Susan's help I would be able to paint every day on Nantucket, where the light was silvery and picturesque subject matter abounded.

"Be sure to be here for cocktails tomorrow at 12:30," my father-in-law said emphatically as we were saying good night. "The Harveys will be coming—everyone on Nantucket wants to meet you both. We are going to the Robinsons across the street on Monday. And then, Henry, on Tuesday the Rivers from San Francisco, parents and children, will be here for a week at the Woodbox on Pleasant Street."

"I hope you'll be spending lots of time with the newly wed Tracy and Joan Rivers," Mary added. "Your husband, Olga, went to kindergarten with Tracy. His wife, Joan, is a daughter of the Timberlakes from Piedmont. Joan is lovely, you'll like her. Olga, we want you as much as possible to meet the daughters of our old friends from San Francisco. Some of them will in time become your lifelong friends. Next winter at Christmas you'll have to bring Michael to San Francisco."

Promising to return the next day at exactly 12:30, we set forth across the garden for the Barn behind 75 Main Street. The garden between the two houses, Henry Coffin's pride, had once been worked on diligently by his wife Mary Swift. Oversize pale hydrangeas could be made out against the old brick wall at the back of it. Recently planted by Henry Senior, a privet hedge was in full silver bloom. Silently, Henry Coffin's pear trees with their contorted limbs seemed to be urging us to stop, to linger in the darkness. But the lawn underfoot was wet with evening dew, and we hurried past the ivy-grown carriage house toward the wooden gate at the back of the garden.

Outside the air smelled of the ocean, it felt like satin against the skin. I proposed a walk before sending the baby-sitter home. We could perhaps walk to the beach at Brant Point, where a tiny lighthouse signals the entrance of Nantucket harbor. But Henry said that it had been a long day. We went straight to the Barn and sent young Susan home.

As soon as she left, Henry said in a low, definitive voice. "You of course do as you like, you may want to stay on with Michael, but as far as I am concerned I'll fly back to New York tomorrow. I warn you: Tracy Rivers has to be one of the most boring people on earth. I don't care for the nonsense that lies ahead—the Harveys, the Robinsons, the Rivers. I have only two weeks' vacation every year, I was hoping to explore Nantucket in peace. I am going home."

I knew even then that this was an important moment in our relationship with the senior Carlisles—I myself was not looking forward to a holiday populated with Harveys and Robinsons. For having met some of the Carlisles' friends over the months, I suspected that they seldom spoke of anything that might be of interest to me. I was tempted to say: "Yes, let's go home," and help Henry loosen his ties with his parents. But it seemed wrong somehow— or were my motives self-serving? Why separate Michael from his grandparents? And from myself, whom they liked? My father-in-law was such a nice man! The idea that he would create a painting studio on Nantucket touched me deeply. This successful engineer took my avocation seriously. I said to Henry, "I know how short your holiday is. Tomorrow you'll do as you want. But now let's have a look at last year's old barn."

The dilapidated horse barn which we had explored on our first visit, admiring its beams, the fine proportions of its hayloft, was now a summerhouse. With the help of a local carpenter, George Hamblin, who had come out of retirement to help him, Henry

Senior had redesigned the barn, leaving only the old plank walls as they were. Downstairs he had created a small sitting room to one side. Next to it, a kitchen had been built behind a high counter, where the horse stalls had once been. A cardboard sign bearing the name of a horse was still nailed to the planks: "Tom," it said.

Upstairs, where hay had once been kept, there were now two bedrooms. Michael was sleeping in the smaller one. The other was spacious, with a high ceiling and windows all around the room. It was furnished like a painter's loft, with a brand new double bed and a worktable covered with a Polynesian tapa cloth borrowed from the attic. An ancient carved Chinese easel stood in the middle of the room. Downstairs in the sitting room a wood fire was burning in the fireplace. Mollified, Henry made us a nightcap. "I do like what Dad and George Hamblin have done here," he said. "I guess somehow we will manage to evade the dreary Rivers."

CHAPTER FIFTEEN

Summer Pleasures

The next morning we were wakened by a muffled commotion outside the barn. Henry Senior had warned us that he and George Hamblin, who was helping him reshingle the barn, would be starting work at eight in the morning. At the sound of the hammering Michael rushed outside in his pajamas and inspected the pack of new shingles that looked like oversized wooden cookies stacked up against a wall. Then he tried out the heavy hammer that was lying in the grass. Henry Senior retrieved it swiftly and good-humoredly. He was dressed in working clothes—old khaki pants, a flannel plaid shirt, a paint-splattered canvas hat. Then he set up an aluminum ladder against the side of the Barn. He and I joined efforts in keeping Michael from ascending it. Finally the ladder was laid down in the grass, and Michael busied himself with the shingles.

My father-in-law was a tall, heavyset man with an elongated face who resembled other Coffins in the family portraits at 75 Main Street. Like his relatives, he had blue eyes and a fleshy chin, but he lacked their solemnity: he moved with small, efficient movements. Not long before, a heart attack had forced him to curtail his work as a mining consultant. He made up for this by working furiously on the restoration of his grandfather's house. This was his way of forestalling anxiety—he shared with his ancestors that tense look, which is often seen in American nineteenth-century portraits.

Now at last there was time for Henry Senior to do everything he wanted—work on the family house in Nantucket, explore the moors, visit with the islanders, some of whom he had known since childhood, join their small and eccentric local club, the Wharf Rat Club, and get to know the new "summer people." Henry Senior involved himself in all of this enthusiastically.

High on a ladder George Hamblin was already at work. With a heavy iron hook he pulled off the old rotten shingles from the Barn's walls. Michael watched him in fascination. The tearing sound as the old nails gave way was singular and soul rending. George worked on, a quiet man in blue overalls and a baseball cap. His round steel-rimmed glasses gave him an air of extreme gravity. He too, like Henry Senior, moved with purposeful movements. As we were introduced he came down his perch and shook hands with us ceremoniously and took us back inside the Barn. He wanted to point out the scrollwork he had installed along the staircase there. It was in keeping with the Nantucket tradition of decorative restraint and yet it was joyous, a pattern of waves ascending from the first to the second floor.

George was pleased to be a part of the restoration of one of Nantucket's patriarchal homes. Soon 75 Main Street would be as good as new, he told us. As a child he remembered seeing Henry Coffin strolling down Main Street, a majestic white-haired man who liked to get his daily newspaper himself. George Hamblin descended from a long line of carpenters whose tireless, anonymous efforts had preserved Nantucket town after it had become impoverished. For the smallest of wages, year after year, these craftsmen had maintained the town as it had looked in the 1850s, when the tide of Nantucket's fortunes had begun to recede.

We went out again, and just in time. Michael had picked up George's iron hook and had gone on to help himself to a can of nails left at the foot of the ladder. My father-in-law looked nervous. Fortunately young Susan came up to the Barn's gate just then, ready to take Michael to the beach. Henry, Jr., went across the street to study the logbooks in the attic of 75 Main Street. I went back into the Barn to unpack our clothes. As I washed the breakfast dishes I once again admired Henry Senior's ingenuity. What a practical kitchen, and how inviting the shiny new pots and pans, the "blue onion" china! Upstairs I looked at the thick terry cloth towels, the rugs, the expensive new beds. It all was quite luxurious compared to our flat on Gramercy Park.

As I made the beds, I composed paintings in my head. Here was a corner window opening onto bright green lawns enclosed by picket fences, apple trees framing the view to the right. One could set a still life in front of the window on that diminutive round table, or else pick one of the late-summer roses in the garden and place it directly on the ledge in a glass. The antique Chinese easel looked functional despite the carved dragons climbing its legs.

I liked the new Barn, but I also had a sense of loss. I had wanted to come back to Nantucket to try to find the past there—Henry's past, America's past. But now that past, which had shone forth so clearly on our previous visit to the island, was obscured by layers of thick blankets and towels and chintz curtains, by the dazzling sunshine outside. I had to find a copy of *Moby-Dick* and reread it. Two of his forebears were saturized in it, Henry had said: the two sanctimonious Quaker merchants who come aboard the *Pequod* before she sails off were undoubtedly inspired by sailors' tales about Henry and Charles Coffin that Melville would have heard even before he came to Nantucket.

Henry's father had moved to San Francisco, escaping the strictures of life in New England. I knew that he had, fallen in love with the romance of the West especially after reading Mark Twain's *Roughing It*. He had had a successful career in San Francisco. Still he had been a newcomer there. Was the feeling of repressed anxiety he projected due to that transition? Was young Henry himself as much of a carefree Californian as he maintained? It would be helpful to know more about all of this—I might be a better mother to Michael if I did.

I moved closer to the corner window in the bedroom and looked out at the neighbors' apple trees, at their summer daylilies and climbing roses, a combination of bright orange and shocking pink typical of Nantucket, which I was often to use in my pictures in the years to come. I could see Henry Senior and George Hamblin working away at the side of the Barn just below me. They worked together rhythmically. My father-in-law make a comradely tone as he spoke with George. Was this a kinship between two men from Nantucket or the result of Henry Senior's experience as a mining engineer? For all his Republican convictions, my father-in-law was a democratically minded man, as befits a true Yankee.

As I finished putting our clothes away in the Barn's ample closets, there was time before cocktails at 12:30 to run down to the small town beach known locally as the Children's Beach. I had my heart set on a swim with Michael. The day was hot, with a hint of fall in the clear sunshine. Nantucket was quiet and yet festive, with a small shell and basket shop, a makeshift postcard stand to remind one that it was a summer resort.

On the way to the beach I passed a truck laden with vegetables and flowers parked under the elms halfway down Main Street. An elderly man with bright blue eyes was selling corn and huge ripe tomatoes and bunches of dahlias almost as brilliant as those I had bought on the day of Henry's first visit to Le Plessis. A line of women waiting to be served chatted quietly. They all wore a kind of uniform—blouses with small round collars, wraparound denim skirts, moccasins. The children they held by the hand were well-behaved. Men in Bermuda shorts passed each other with friendly nods.

The elms of Main Street, planted in the 1850s by Henry Coffin and his brother Charles, spread violet shadows across the wide, honey-colored street. After New York with its crowds sweltering in the heat, this seemed a safe, old-fashioned universe as would have existed before the dreadful First World War of my parents' childhood. It was hard to believe that, on a chilly April evening the year before, I had fancied seeing Ishmael himself hurrying by on Lower Main Street.

The harbor at the end of Main Street sheltered a half dozen sailboats swaying in the light wind. Here was North Wharf, with its rows of toylike boathouses. To the left, Children's Beach was half hidden by clumps of wild roses in bloom. In the distance I could make out Michael and Susan sitting under a striped beach umbrella. The water sparkled, children were playing in the shallow water. A small boy in green shorts flew a kite shaped like a butterfly. The round clock of the Unitarian Church showed eleven o'clock. I fell in love with Children's Beach on that day. For many years afterward, before its waters became polluted, it would be the outdoor studio where I read or sketched while Michael played at the water's edge.

Leaving Michael and Susan to dry in the sun after a splashy swim,

I hurried back to the Barn. Henry had just returned from the attic across the street. He had been reading Henry Coffin's journals about his voyage to Madeira in 1833. "That was my great-grandfather's only trip away from Nantucket," he said. "His ancestors had been the great American sailors of their age, but Henry Coffin stayed home all his life."

"I can hardly blame him, his house is so very comfortable," I said.

Henry had excused himself from the noontime gathering at 75 Main Street. He would borrow his father's Jeep to go exploring the island on his own.

I took a quick shower in the bathroom of the Barn, a mixture of gleaming appliances, fluffy towels, and old beams. I kept thinking about the uniformed ladies on Main Street and those at the beach who wore strange-looking flowered bathing suits with little skirts. What should I wear in this new environment? The only blouse I had brought had large red-and-white checks and an open collar. My cotton skirt was black and narrowly cut. I owned no moccasins. In addition to my sneakers, which were quite worn, the only shoes I had with me were a pair of black patent leather Italian sandals with high heels.

Then I remembered that I had brought my favorite navy blue polka-dotted summer dress bought at the outdoor market in Le Plessis after the war. It had the Dior look of the late forties, a small waist, a flounced skirt. It would look perfect with the new sandals. I dressed hastily and rushed to 75 Main Street. "How sweet you look," my mother-in-law said as I came in through the garden door. "I am planning to take you shopping this afternoon. We'll get you some moccasins, a tailored blouse, a denim skirt. . . . And surely you'll want to have the kind of bathing suit we all prefer out here—a dressmaker suit with an overskirt."

The idea of my wearing a suit with a skirt struck me as absurd. At that moment and once and for all, I decided that, at my age, I would not be told what to wear by anyone, on Nantucket or any-where else. I was still a Parisienne. And in fact Mary respected my show of independence. Little by little as the conformism of the Eisenhower era faded away we became good friends.

CHAPTER SIXTEEN

In Search of Clams

The morning set for a tour of the island was again sunny and still. Henry Senior came over to the Barn after breakfast. Michael and Susan had left for the beach. The big umbrella had been hoisted onto the stroller, which Michael insisted on pushing along the sidewalk himself. Henry, Jr., had gone off to the attic across the street. My father-in-law was full of news: "The Rivers will be here in the late afternoon! Elizabeth is cooking lobsters for dinner. Olga, you and I have a project. I think that, in addition to the lobsters, we should have clams for the guests. The tide will be low at two o'clock. As we drive around the island, we'll stop at Madeket and go clamming. On the way we'll see the beach where Tristram Coffin landed. He now has descendants in the hundreds of thousands all over America, and your husband is one of them!"

On Liberty Street, where his Jeep was parked, Henry Senior was loading wire baskets with large round corks attached to them as markers, and wicked-looking rusty rakes that resembled those devils brandished on medieval paintings. His Jeep was a big boxy station wagon christened for one of the Coffin whalers, its name *Speedwell* was carefully lettered on the door. As we drove across town on Siasconset Road the baskets and the rakes rattled cheerfully in the back.

Out of town, the beauty of the morning took my breath away. Late summer wildflowers bloomed along the road, a creamy mixture of blue chickoree and pink soap flowers—as we called them in Le

Plessis. These were overlaid with Queen Anne's lace, breaking along the edge of the road in foamy waves. The sky grew huge, and the earth was a soft green, touched with gold here and there. As far as one could see, low-lying hills were covered with dwarf evergreens and curly wild vines. Driving along briskly, my father-in-law spoke over the rattling: "These are the moors, we call them Commons, lands once held collectively by the islanders for sheep grazing and haying. I very much hope they will never be developed. That would be against every Nantucket tradition."

We followed the edge of a large pond dotted with seagulls resting on the water's surface like scattered pearls. The ocean beyond it gleamed. "This is Sacachacha Pond," Henry Senior said, and he pulled off the road and stopped. As we got out, a flock of seagulls took flight with an outburst of angry screeching. "The sandbar between the pond and the ocean is a perfect place to swim," Henry Senior said. "Here, depending on how the wind blows, you might settle by the pond or else by the ocean. The sandy roads we have just passed are public accesses to the beach. On Nantucket, leaving free passage to the water is an old, highly respected custom."

I wished we could have taken the very next road to the sea— Henry Senior called them ruts. I would have liked to see the two sides of Sacachacha Pond, or rather its four elements—sand, sky, pond, ocean—that were mingling and glistening in the distance. But the pond with the scratchy Indian name disappeared. We were now in sight of a lighthouse striped in black and white, standing like a huge toy near the edge of a grassy bluff overlooking the ocean. "Sankety Head," Henry Senior called out. "On a dark night one can see its light sweeping across the garden at Seventy-five Main Street. And here is the golf course established by a Coffin first cousin who remained on the island and was able to put his share of land to good use."

The road followed the bluff, which curved westward. After a while, as it became less precipitous, Henry Senior stopped Speedwell and manipulated its gears, putting it in four-wheel drive. We were going to go down and drive directly on the beach along the south shore. Madeket, where we would be looking for clams, was at the other end of the island, another twelve miles away. I had never in my life ridden on a beach before. I had a sense of weightlessness as the car rushed along the water's edge, where small silver waves came to die in lacy scrolls. There was not a soul to be seen. Seagulls and terns darted up from a mirrorlike sea as we neared them.

A half hour later, just as the movement was beginning to make me drowsy, Henry Senior stopped abruptly. "Two o'clock, the tide is at its lowest just now. What with your help we'll get plenty of clams for supper! There is a bed here, which I discovered a year ago. I was driving along and decided to have a swim, and here were all these clams underfoot! Naturally I keep it a secret from everyone on the island; that's the way it has always been on Nantucket—absolute secrecy about fishing and hunting spots."

We had reached Madeket, a succession of coves and of small rounded dunes covered with beach grass and stunted pine trees jutting out into a turquoise sea. "The clams should be right here, that clump of dwarf pines is my landmark," Henry Senior said. We carried those devilish-looking rakes and the baskets down into the water until it was waist high. We started scraping the bottom of the sea, bringing the rakes up as they filled with gravel and seaweed. More often than not, mixed in with the pebbles a clam would be there. Sometimes two or three were caught in one scoop. They were of varying sizes—the tiny ones were thrown back. The big ones Henry Senior called cherrystones, the smaller ones, littlenecks, but they were the same species of shellfish.

At once I discovered a way to clam without using the rake, with its heavy oversize handle. I could spot live clams at the bottom of the sea. Half buried in sand, they looked whiter than dead seashells. All I had to do was bend down and pick them up.

In less than an hour we had filled the baskets marked by corks that started to strain and wobble—the tide was rising. A sharp wind came up from the sea. "Time to go," Henry Senior said. Suddenly the water felt very cold. I could barely drag our rakes up the beach as Henry Senior carried ashore the heavy baskets. He could not contain his enthusiasm as we loaded Speedwell and wrapped ourselves in dry towels. "It must be your childhood on that other island, Olga! You are a great clammer! Now we have not only enough clams for hors d'oeuvres tonight, but we can also make chowder with the big ones, the cherrystones. We'll use the middle-size ones for clams gourmet. It's an old San Francisco recipe, clams on the half-shell broiled with bits of bacon, parsley, and lemon juice. We'll get Elizabeth to make these tomorrow!"

Still wrapped in our towels, we proudly carried the baskets of clams through the back door of 75 Main Street. Mary Carlisle was ensconced on the sofa in the back parlor, doing a crossword puzzle. When she saw us there, standing barefoot with our dripping baskets she cried out, "Goodness gracious!" She looked distressed. Getting up from the couch she said in a depressed voice, "What am I to do with all these *dead* clams? Dearie, the icebox is already filled with *dead* lobsters! I would be ever so much happier if you had let Elizabeth make us her Irish stew for tonight! Now we'll have all these smelly lobster shells lying in the basement till Wednesday, when the garbage man comes. Do what you will with the clams, but don't bring them into the house. Also, you are both walking around with sandy feet."

"You mustn't worry about the lobster shells. I will take the trash to the dump tomorrow myself," said Henry Senior sheepishly as he put the baskets out on the porch. "As for the clams, they aren't in the least *dead*. I guess perhaps we should take them to the Barn. Olga, what do you think, is there room enough in the icebox there?"

I hastened to say that there was. I felt sorry for Henry Senior. Suddenly he looked silly in his beach towel accoutrement. We carried the two baskets across Liberty Street. The clams barely fit in the lower compartment of the refrigerator. "Please don't worry, Henry and I love clams," I said. "If you think Mary won't mind, we'll open a few and bring them over on a platter for hors d'oeuvres when we come over for dinner."

"Wonderful, wonderful," Henry Senior said. "I have an idea. Tomorrow, if you agree, we'll make clam chowder and clams gourmet right here in the Barn. Do you know that though I designed this kitchen I never have used it, not even to boil an egg? It will be fun to try it out!"

"Henry, Jr., likes to cook," I said. "We'll help you make the clam chowder. And—Henry, I do like Nantucket!"

This new island was beautiful, it was evocative of my childhood island, but not enough to make me feel nostalgic. My friendship with the two Henrys, different as they were from each other, made Nantucket feel safe.

CHAPTER SEVENTEEN

Maria Mitchell

One evening that summer, Henry invited me to go "laning" with him. We held hands as we walked along the grassy lanes that weave a web of leafy alleyways all around Nantucket Town, linking one street to another. The gardens overflowing with honeysuckle and late summer roses were dark, but the bleached-out, shingled gray houses shone faintly in the moonlight. We peered into parlors, with their austere furnishings—brick fireplaces where whole meals were once cooked on wood fires; spindly chairs painted black, and nautical prints on discretely patterned, papered walls.

"These empty rooms are eerie," I said. "Where are the people? Are they watching television in the back of the house? Reading in bed? What a life it must have been for the women here: waiting for the men to return from their voyages year after year! How could they stand it?"

"They did, very well," Henry said. "The very first Quaker leader on the island was a woman, Mary Starbuck. She helped establish her religion on Nantucket. I think her house is still standing somewhere nearby. It was called Parliament House: people gathered at Mary Starbuck's to discuss religion and politics. At the time of the Salem witch hunts on the mainland, a few families with Quaker backgrounds fled to Nantucket to escape persecutions by the Boston Puritans. As the men went out to sea on ever longer sea voyages women learned to take charge. And they had time to educate themselves. America's first woman astronomer, Maria Mitchell, was born and brought up on the island. You should read her biography; it's in Dad's library. Maria Mitchell would have been a distant cousin of Henry Coffin's. She was a very interesting woman.

"There is another book there that might amuse you," Henry added with a smile, "by a Frenchman named Crevecoeur. Impressed as he was by the harmonious social life among the Nantucket Quakers at the end of the eighteenth century, Crevecoeur did note that, every afternoon around five o'clock, the ladies of Nantucket were in the habit of taking a little laudanum as they drank tea in their parlors. That was opium, easily available in those days in a seaport trading with the whole world. Taverns and brothels along the waterfront served dubious characters like Queequog."

Following darkened lanes, we were looking for the "three bricks," the merchants' houses on Upper Main Street (built in the 1830s) that are famed on the island for their elegance. Indeed, that evening they looked like jewels, their rose-colored walls gleaming against the white woodwork. We walked on and on. I had no idea of how large a town Nantucket was. In Melville's days, it had been a huge seaport, with a population of almost ten thousand, Henry said.

"Nantucket was a microcosm of America for a time," said Henry. "Quakers were against capital punishment long before Tolstoy. They were remarkably progressive in some ways, especially the lapsed Quakers, like Maria Mitchell."

It was time to get back to the Barn, to the fluffy blankets and comfortable beds, perfect for lovemaking. Even more inviting were the canopied beds at 75 Main Street, but they were inaccessible except on those rare occasions when the Carlisles went out for lunch or dinner. As a rule the house was a beehive of activities well into the night.

Regardless of the hour, Henry Senior would suddenly say, "Dearie, I have an idea," and then would suggest some improvement destined to make everyday life ever more comfortable in the ancestral home. My mother-in-law was likely to sigh at the prospect of more commotion, yet she would be tolerant. As days went by, the ancient front door bell pull was rewired, a dumbwaiter turned into a laundry shoot, an upstairs fireplace unsealed and made usable again.

The next day I found Maria Mitchell's biography in Henry Senior's library, made up for the most part of books about whaling. In the days that followed I read it on the beach, where Michael and I spent a good part of each day.

Nantucket had nurtured a woman mathematician who had had a passion for observing the stars. She discovered a comet and was acclaimed as a world-famous astronomer while she was still in her twenties. Later she taught astronomy at Vassar and traveled in Italy with the Hawthornes. She had been a freethinker. After her death, most of her journals were destroyed by an overzealous sister under the pretense that "Maria would have wanted it." That sister, Phoebe, was guilty of a great crime, because Maria Mitchell had had an original mind and a great gift for words. What was collected in that somewhat fulsome biography said what I needed to hear that summer. To discover that Nantucket had a tradition of female accomplishment was exciting. Here was an American legacy that I should try to make my own.

Maria Mitchell warned against the limitations that women impose upon themselves: "Until women throw off reverence for authority they will never develop." She spoke about one's larger responsibilities as well: "It is frightful to commit a sin alone, and few do it. We prop ourselves with accomplices; we surround ourselves with those who can drown in us the uprising of conscience." And, "Doing is comparatively easy, as long as you remember that there are no ready-made laws for your individual case." And then, "Oh women, lift your heads from your laps! Look around you! Face the light!"

Inspired by an islander of another time who seemed to welcome me to her island, that summer I worked every day. The Barn was a fine place to paint in the afternoons. Maple trees planted a century before kept it cool. I remember one such afternoon vividly. It was a moment of clarity, it was about painting, my guiding Quaker Inner Light, light itself captured with paints on canvas.

I was working on a still life placed against the corner window of the studio, an arrangement of a late-summer rose and cherries against a backdrop of old apple trees. Suffused with the late afternoon light, the painting was turning out well.

The Barn was quiet except for a bee buzzing now and then, bumping softly against the screen of the open window. Across Liberty Street, Michael was playing with Mary in the garden of 75 Main Street. Faintly their voices reached me. Every afternoon Michael came back from visiting his grandmother in excellent spirits. Freshly scrubbed, he would appear in a new outfit—corduroy coveralls with appliqué bears, or a tiny Lacoste shirt that made him look quite grown-up. He loved the orderly life at 75 Main Street. From the beginning he shared the elder Carlisles' appreciation of earthly comforts. That afternoon, knowing that he was content helped me concentrate on the cherries and the beautiful Peace rose.

That evening, glancing at the picture standing in a corner of the studio, Henry said, "Say, this is good, when did you do it?" I looked, and indeed the rose and cherries on the canvas fairly glowed while the still life on the window ledge was beginning to disintegrate, the full rose shedding its petals, the cherries eaten, with only a few pits on the edge of the saucer to remind one of their existence.

Henry and I still go back to Nantucket in the summer. I know of no better place to paint than the big house, which we share with Henry's brother now that the senior Carlisles have died. As for the Barn, it has lost its view of apple trees to development. Young millionaires from Boston, Washington, and New York have chosen the island for their vacations. Nantucket Town has grown wildly, its gardens a maze of pergolas, decorative fences, and pavilions, which make laning difficult. The dunes are dotted with mock Tudor mansions—there is no zoning on the island beyond the center of town. But 75 Main Street remains a peaceful realm where one of Henry Coffin's pear trees still thrives. Mary Swift's hydrangeas can be found in midsummer, and Henry Senior's privet hedges, grown to dizzying heights, keep the outside world at bay.

CHAPTER EIGHTEEN

The New York Art Scene

Henry returned to New York first, suntanned and ready to confront Alfred and Blanche Knopf and the challenges of New York publishing. Michael and I stayed on in the Barn for another two weeks. When we returned, New York seemed carefree after the island town with the fence-girdled houses like prim dowagers wearing pearls. Or so it seemed at first: soon I realized that a major revolution in painting was underway and that I had crucial decisions to make. On Nantucket thanks to Maria Mitchell, I had had a confirmation of what I would do with my life, but I had no idea of what my paintings would be like. I only knew that they would have to come from within, from some region inaccessible to the conscious mind. This was the secret shared by the art students of those days: "one had to learn how to express one's emotion through painting." It was a forceful injunction in New York—I had never heard anyone recommend such a thing in Paris. Little by little, I discovered that it was an American concept, derived in part from one of Maria Mitchell's New England friends, Ralph Waldo Emerson, who had occasionally lectured on Nantucket. In the European artistic tradition, only Van Gogh, who was sometimes considered insane, had spoken of emotions as being central in the creation of paintings.

Manhattan helped me put my doubts aside about painting. As I walked the crowded midtown streets or rode the bus to classes at Hunter College where I had enrolled that fall, I no longer felt like a stranger in the city. It was not only the warm weather that lingered, I felt sure of myself: if painting as practiced at Hunter dissatisfied me, I would do it on my own.

The light in our Gramercy Park living room, with its walls painted a deep green, was beautiful in the mornings, the yellowing trees of the park belted by a spiky, neo-Gothic grille waiting to be painted. The museums and their treasures amassed by enlightened philanthropists, the food markets on the lower West side were the promise of a future in art. Walking with Michael, clutching his hand firmly—he was adventurous and often tried to escape into a wider world—I wandered along New York's carnival streets which might have been painted by a Dutch master. At the end of the day Michael and I returned to Henry, to the safety of our emerald green nest on Granerey Park.

In the mornings I took Michael to a small prekindergarten on nearby Irving Place. He fell in love at once with his teacher there, Miss Stone, almost as plump and as jolly as Susan on Nantucket. I spent hours sketching, studying the sedate clusters of nursemaids and children framed by the crowded streets. Like Montsouris, little by little the park became populated with imaginary presences summoned by its Victorian outlines. I almost could see them. I was still reading Henry James's novels.

In James were intimations of secrets that I did not quite wish to probe to the end, the opaque language making this all too easy. Still, my English was improving, I could follow the novels' plots, and they were giving me a key to the Anglo-Saxon world into which I had married. This was a key I didn't quite want to use but one I liked to have nonetheless, just in case. In fact I owe Henry James a great debt. Over the years, slowly he helped me decipher certain aspects of my new life and understand situations, touching on matters of money and sex, that would have otherwise remained incomprehensible to me because of my parents' idealism, their lack of money, and their liberal outlook on society.

As for art, having failed to do justice to the trees of Montsouris, I wanted to learn to draw those in the park across the street. The practice of painting, like music, demands enormous persistence: it takes a lifetime to learn to draw a tree. I read somewhere that in his brief tenure as a teacher, Matisse suggested to his pupils that they line their canvases against the wall and find in them that which is uniquely theirs, and then try to develop it in their work. To some degree I was eventually able to do this, but only over decades of work and of museum-going. Slowly I learned to allow myself to paint as I did in childhood, without preconceived notions, as wise Zen monks recommend.

In particular, I would not be shaped by the art that was being produced just then, and especially not by that lively newborn, the revolutionary New York School of Abstract Expressionism, which was asserting itself brashly in the pages of *Art News* as the painters' only future. *Art News* was a magazine read from cover to cover every month with an almost religious fervor by my schoolmates at Hunter.

Studying it with a mixture of curiosity and awe, I thought of Mayakovsky's menacing words as he had tried—vainly as it turned out—to maintain himself at the helm of the Soviet avant-garde in the late twenties: "Woe to those who are pushed off the ship of modernity!" Yet my pictures owed a great deal to what was done around me—the loose brushwork, the primary colors, and especially the dream of someday learning to discover how to project my innermost feelings—my very self—directly onto the canvas.

In those years, Abstract Expressionism was not only a school of painting, it was an ideology that the artist needed to embrace if he "wanted his work to count," as the phrase went. Intolerant of other styles, it echoed the aggressive artistic dogmatism that had reigned elsewhere, that of whimsical Dada in France and of stodgy Soviet Socialist Realism. Its practitioners maintained that they had reached an esthetic plateau. Their way of painting was the ultimate one, suspended in an everlasting present, destined somehow to remain forever appropriate. It was like attaining the ideal state of Communism in a socialist state. The absence of recognizable subject matter allegedly conferred on Abstract Expressionism an enigmatic timelessness.

Every week I went to the Museum of Modern Art, grateful for its wider acceptance of modernism. Bonnard had died only five years before, he was—almost—a contemporary. His green and golden breakfast scene was a vision of France as Paradise. I studied Matisse's pink garden table with a basket of ivy on it that had recently appeared there; the little boy playing the piano in a soft Parisian gray light which so exactly recreated my own exasperation with music lessons as a child. These pictures were being assembled by an American scholar, Alfred Barr: he was putting France within New Yorkers' reach. I took this to mean that there was a future to painting regardless of fashion. These were only the fifties, the end of the millenium was a half century away, yet I believed that Bonnard's lighthearted wish would come true: "I'd like to arrive before the young painters of the year 2000 on butterfly wings." In Paris in the late forties, my mother and I had been deeply moved by his last painting, the almond tree in bloom against an ultramarine sky.

From the museum, which had not yet been given its Freudian nickname, MOMA, I walked up to Fifty-seventh Street. Along the way several galleries had Joseph Cornell's boxes for sale. These were small, three-dimensional collages, dark and self-contained. They pulled one powerfully into their depths. Someone at Hunter said that the magician who made these lived in Queens, that one could go there by subway and call on him. But I never went, nor did I have the hundred dollars that such a box might cost. Much as I wanted one, I took comfort in knowing that possessing one might cause its magic to vanish. Or else the box would start expanding, trying to invade one's life, like the Jamesian characters whom I kept at a distance behind the iron grille of Gramercy Park.

Usually I took Michael with me to the Museum of Modern Art. He loved our expeditions, the ride on the bus, the people around us. While I looked at the pictures masterfully assembled by Alfred Barr, Michael explored the museum on his own and studied the museum goers. Often he engaged them in conversation in a manner so urbane that I did not have the heart to stop him. Perhaps I should have tried to discourage his unremitting sociability, but then we never stayed very long at the museum. I communed with the Bonnard and the Matisses, then on the way home we stopped in a coffee shop for Michael's supper. The New York coffee shops of those years were cozy, the waiters brusque but genial, the bland foods a small child's choice.

There we discussed the events of the day, our encounters, the city about us, which was being rebuilt at that time, cranes towering all around us. Michael was a kind, seductive child, and our outings usually turned into triumphal marches punctuated by admiring glances and comments from strangers on the street. The world loved Michael. I thought of Alphonse Daudet's tale about the little she-goat in the mountains of Provence and prayed that he might never meet his bad wolf: "*Les genêts d'or s'ouvraient à son passage et sentaient bon tant qu'ils pouvaient.*" "Golden blooms opened as she passed by and smelled as deliciously as they could."

As far as my own pursuits were concerned, I made it easy on myself: Michael's interests, as far as I could figure them out, came first. Even Henry, even painting were secondary. This was a sim-pleminded rule that allowed me to navigate New York's uncharted waters with a measure of self-assurance. Because of this rule I felt no urge to have more children. Neither did Henry, most probably for the same unspoken reason: they would have made life too complicated to handle gracefully for two individuals from such different backgrounds as ours.

I began to get to know some of the students in my painting class at Hunter, even though in their eyes I was odd, a visitor from some faraway land. Depending on their backgrounds, it would be Gay Paree, or the past, the Old Country, the Russia that some of them liked for having read her classics. Many among them had eastern European Jewish roots, though there were also people of Irish and Italian descent and Hispanics who had come by way of Los Angeles. Motherwell was becoming well known: students from all over the United States started coming to Hunter's graduate art department especially to study with him.

Every Monday night after class he invited three or four students to go with him to an Irish bar on Third Avenue and Sixty-fifth Street for a beer and a hamburger. One evening that fall he asked me to join the group. I was flattered and soon discovered how satisfying a cool Lowenbrau could be after three hours spent in the stifling, fluorescent-lit studio, where the air was heavy with the smell of house paints. Inexpensive, fluid, easy to handle, these lead-based paints created the much-desired flat surfaces favored by art students. Their danger had not yet been established, though in those years artists who used them complained of headaches and dizziness, which were blamed on the intensity of the creative process.

The bar that Motherwell patronized was dark and divided up into deep booths upholstered in blood red leatherette. There we could sit as long as we wished. The waiter with the caressing Irish voice became our friend. I had never quite identified an Irish accent before. Once when I came home I picked up Henry's Modern Library edition of Yeats's poems. Their music seized me. Though I could never hope to be able to speak or write it faultlessly, I was in love with the English language, its richness almost as heady as that of painting.

The conversations in the Irish bar were almost exclusively about painting, conducted in that intense, colloquial painters' jargon that irritated Henry whenever he met my fellow students. However, more often than not, it was Motherwell who told us stories during these outings, in his soft-spoken, literate, California-bred English, which was very much like Henry's.

He told us about the French Surrealists, newcomers to America who had befriended him in New York when he was a young man learning to paint. Peggy Guggenheim, ever so rich and wild and married briefly to the Surrealist Max Ernst, had given Motherwell his first show in her gallery, Art of this Century. She had also launched Jackson Pollock, and now these two artists were the leaders of the Action Painters, a term recently coined by the critic Harold Rosenberg to describe the New York Abstract Expressionists.

Motherwell was in his early forties then. He had been born in San Francisco, in a family that must have resembled the Carlisles, though perhaps wealthier: his father had been a Wells Fargo banker. Motherwell was tall and patrician looking and had sandy blond hair. Unexpectedly, a smile would fill his rounded face with kindness, dissolving momentarily the masculine stiffness of the well-bred American. As he spoke he tilted his head ever so slightly in a way that made him look vulnerable. There was an aura of sadness about him. A friendship developed between us little by little. As a rule, Motherwell was affable to all until the bimonthly painting critiques. Then he would put down mercilessly the less talented—or were they less imitative?—among us.

During these critiques Motherwell would suddenly become angry. It was as if he could not reconcile himself with the fact his manner of painting might not be the ultimate one in the history of art. I remember him saying sadly, more to himself than to us: "One must try to remember that no one—no one at all—will ever be missed in this world after death. I can never forget it, this is my dark side."

Trying to conquer this darkness, feverishly, Motherwell was engaged in formulating the tenets of Abstract Expressionism, which was taking over the economics and the taste of the art community in New York. Paintings by the acknowledged masters of the previous decades—George Bellows, Thomas Hart Benton, Reginald March—were disappearing from museums and galleries, to be replaced by nonfigurative paintings and sculptures. Even the works of the committed modernists of the past decade, including those of Georgia O'Keeffe, surely one of America's most inventive artists, were ridiculed. It mattered little to the New York modernists that O'Keeffe was an abstractionist in the full sense of that word, seeking to reveal in her pictures the abstracted essence of both the natural and the man-made worlds. Clement Greenberg, one of the high priests of the new movement, had condemned her unconditionally: "... the greatest part of her work adds up to little more than tinted photography [which has] less to do with art than with private worship and the embellishment of private fetishes with secret and arbitrary meanings." In my case, when Norman Mailer asked me the meaning of my painting flowers I had the presence of mind to say that they stood for sex, which pleased him.

Indeed, a radically new approach to the visual arts was being promoted among the New York artists, and Motherwell was its most articulate spokesman. Art was no longer concerned with trivial, personal matters. Recognizable subject matter had become obsolete in pictures, which had to reflect the artist's innermost self by means of nonfigurative forms.

Unwilling to forsake the visible world, I held my own silently, bringing to class, week after week, still lifes of artichokes or radishes or crimson beets or onions, whereas students around me worked with house paints on great sheets of Masonite in a style that would have been called *Tachisme* in France right after the war. The vegetables looked forlorn in the unkempt, crowded studio, but I did not know how to begin a painting without a visual starting point. Moreover, this was an opportunity to assert myself as a figurative artist.

Motherwell was tolerant only of those among his pupils who

painted large canvases in the prevalent Abstract Expressionist manner. He hardly ever glanced at my modestly sized paintings, averting
his eyes politely. His silence made it clear that he would have liked
me to give up painting altogether, to become a scholar, perhaps to
translate into English the texts of the French Surrealists, which he
was researching for his scholarly work—he edited texts on modern
art for Viking Press.

I tried to be brave. I ignored him. I was learning all sorts of
useful things in Motherwell's class. One evening he advised me to
lay my canvas flat on the floor as I worked, instead of using an
easel. This simple suggestion helped me break away from a realistic
vision of space, helping me find over the years a personal way to
paint still lifes. Other techniques were suggested by my fellow students. Learning how to take advantage of accidents, of drips and
smudges, was a mannerism cultivated all over New York in those
days.

In the Irish bar, speaking in a low voice with his students who
were in awe of his worldliness, Motherwell allowed as to how he
hated teaching. He did it only because he had a family to support,
his wife Betty and two small daughters. In any case, the vast majority
of the students at Hunter were not painters at all. Why not admit
it? They were taking art courses to be able to meet the requirements
needed to become accredited teachers in the New York school system.

Not so gently Motherwell continued to put down his pupils.
They were parochial, they lacked the most elementary curiosity: for
instance, they lived in New York with its prodigious ethnic diversity,
yet somehow they had never noticed artichokes, though these vegetables, Mediterranean in origin, could be seen in every market in
the city. Those I brought to class had caused a sensation, were they
a flower, a vegetable? How did one eat them? The students who
came to the Irish bar after class were ostensibly the more sophisti-
cated ones in our class, promised perhaps to larger destinies, yet
Motherwell did not hide the fact that, in his opinion, not one of
us was committed enough to painting to become an artist, and this
of course galvanized our energies. We tried hard to become more
singleminded in our work.

At that time the story of how Van Gogh had cut off his ear in a fit of madness, giving it to a prostitute, was a cherished myth among art students, a sign perhaps of the forthcoming acceptance of mind-altering drugs, which were said to help release creative powers. Van Gogh's act of self-mutilation was viewed as the price of artistic triumph. On the other hand, familiarity with basic techniques, including life drawing, was not considered useful to the aspiring painter. In fact it might impede the release of emotions on which Action Painting depended. In the graduate school at Hunter, as far as I know, none of these disciplines were taught at that time.

Much later, when I saw Motherwell in the eighties, it was as if he regretted his early harshness: "I want to go back to teaching," he said. "It is one way to keep learning, to escape the darkness which will conquer sooner or later. Today the young are interested in what I do, and perhaps I can help them find their way."

I said that, as far as I was concerned, his vision of painting as a sacred pursuit had been an inspiration when I was his student. Even his very lack of interest in my work had been helpful, it had toughened me. "Well, yes, you did become a good writer," he said, and we spoke about literature, not about painting. However, as we were saying good-bye he came back to the subject: "Painting is ailing today, and there are no Alfred Barrs, no Harold Rosenbergs...." This was the last conversation we were to have: Robert Motherwell died soon afterward. That year in Nantucket I painted a great deal thinking of him, though the offering of my paintings would have been the last thing he would have wished for.

Back in the fifties, in the course of his long, enthralling monologues, Motherwell recounted how his first wife, a beautiful South American woman, had left him one day without explanation. She had gotten into a car and driven away never to return. He mourned her: Motherwell found all women forever puzzling. We sensed that he had never quite recovered from his first wife's disappearance. Perhaps this tale to which he returned obsessively was his way to exorcise his self-absorption and try to understand the world outside his studio. He would often expound on the inscrutable nature of women.

Wishing to cheer himself and all of us, Motherwell would describe Peggy Guggenheim's fabled parties and those, more modest, given by the impecunious but thoroughly civilized French artists who had come to New York when war had overtaken Europe. They had been his teachers. How delicious their cooking despite their poverty, their joie de vivre both astounding and edifying to an American of Motherwell's background! They had all been there: André Masson, Marc Chagall, Yves Tanguy, Kay Sage, and especially that wizard, the ultimate Dadaist, Marcel Duchamps.

Early on, Motherwell had been the Surrealists' mascot. He had played chess with Duchamps, the master who had given up painting as philosophically trivial. The poets, including André Breton, had been there also, and together they had planted the seeds of the new American art, which was now rising all around us like an irrepressible yeasty dough. Though I considered myself "in the opposition," the fact that painting could matter so much to so many in this enormous city buoyed me.

With a fellow student from Hunter College, Bruce Barton, I went to one of Motherwell's exhibits at the Kootz Gallery on Madison Avenue at Fifty-seventh Street. Motherwell was showing collages there, small ones, though at that time gigantism seemed to be seizing New York—by the late fifties, the enormousness of the pictures heralded the end rather than the birth of an artistic era—only the late Venetians and the French Academicians had routinely painted such vast canvases.

But it was with the late paintings of Monet, with *The Nymphéas* that the Abstract Expressionists identified, not with any dreaded academy—though unbeknownst to themselves, they were in the process of establishing one through their lack of tolerance and especially their ever-widening acceptance into museums that would never be able to sell their works off because so much money would have been invested into their acquisition. They are still there, making the Lili Wallace wing of the otherwise superbly alive Metropolitan Museum feel like a mausoleum, deader even than the Egyptian temple, which is a ghostly enough presence in that museum.

But Motherwell's collages were intimate, made of torn blue Gauloise packages and of brown paper used for mailing by the French publishing house NRF. Against their black backgrounds they were not only decorative, they managed to convey his particular shade of melancholy. I was relieved: works done by an Abstract Expressionist could actually please me. Motherwell's nostalgia for France was infectious. Undertaken at that time, his series *Je t'aime* was genuinely lyrical. Motherwell was paying homage to the plain, everyday voluptuousness of French life.

However, my fellow students at Hunter were more interested in Far Eastern philosophy than in French nostalgia: Paris was no longer the artistic capital of the world, Matisse was dead, Picasso's prodigious fireworks had ceased to impress Americans. In the Irish bar we discussed *Zen and the Art of Archery*, and the recently published books by Allan Watts, which young painters liked to ponder in those years. A new view of the world was being born. If I only listened attentively rather than play the conventional role of a visiting Frenchwoman, which, I suspected, Motherwell wished me to play, I could grasp it despite my imperfect English, which sometimes caused me to lose the thread of the discussion.

In the Zen view of the world causality disappears, living becomes an end in itself. With their solemn simplicity, their frugality, the Zen monks possessed the greatest wisdom: "When you walk, be content to walk. When you are seated, be content to be seated. Above all don't wiggle." In a city where life was becoming ever more hectic, the rents higher, where a majestic-looking old section of warehouses on the West Side was about to be torn down to make room for an ostentatious center dedicated to the arts, students found inspiration in poems that were about living in a perpetual present.

The poet Allen Ginsberg, whom I occasionally encountered at gallery openings, was lecturing people on the need to lead simpler lives. He had just published *Howl*. After Stalin's death, Ginsberg was the first to ask me why I wasn't going to the Soviet Union to help establish there a free worldwide republic of poets and painters.

An ascetic way to live was the lot of many younger artists in the mid-fifties. Richard Bellamy, who ran the Hansa Gallery, earned money as a baby-sitter. Working as a team, Jay Milder and Red Grooms moved furniture for a living. Some artists did substitute teaching at the city's schools, others worked as bartenders at night. For a painter, working on the side was considered a normal thing to do, no one was humiliated by it.

But life was becoming less frugal in New York. Days were fuller and swifter, and yet somehow there was still time for everything—

for housework; for drawing cityscapes in Central Park; for long conversations in the Third Avenue Irish bar; for going out at night to publishers' parties with Henry; for reading Russian bedtime stories to Michael, the ones that had been read to me when I was a child in Paris.

With my parents' encouragement, I persisted in speaking Russian to our son. My parents too spoke Russian to Michael. They were more enterprising than Henry or I when it came to teaching him to ski or to take photographs. Russia was absent from our life, but for my own sake, I wanted to preserve fragments of my legacy. I was in love with Melville and Henry James, with Mark Twain, but Dostoyevsky and Tolstoy remained the masters. One of the great literary experiences of my life would be a collaboration with Henry. In the mid-sixties, together we translated *The Idiot* into English. Henry did not discourage me from teaching Michael Russian and then French. Secretly I dreamed of a trip to France with Michael, so that he might learn French well, and I could visit Aline and Olivier Pagès, with whom I corresponded assiduously.

I remember my winter homecomings from Hunter College on the bus going down Lexington Avenue. It would be almost eleven by then—Henry stayed home with Michael and read manuscripts or wrote while I attended evening graduate classes. A granulous snow would be falling in circles, a great winter storm enveloping the city. Lexington Avenue looked like the bottom of a huge white canyon. The half-empty bus was moving forth steadily, silently. My head, ever so lightly blurred by beer, was full of swirling thoughts about painting and painters. Along Third Avenue the El had been taken down, but the women on the street still dressed as they had in the forties, in Peggy Guggenheim's days—fancy small hats, short jackets, and shoes with very high heels. Winter boots and fur hats had not been discovered—or rediscovered—in New York despite its fierce winters.

Once, when I wore my French boots and a brightly printed scarf around my head, a cab driver scolded me for my careless appearance. To classes I wore pumps and sheer stockings as I trudged in the dark through the snow, bareheaded. But I did not feel the cold, I was composing a still life in my mind. Against a red background

I would paint that small green earthenware pot that I had bought in Collioure almost three years before, and some gray pussy willow branches, a promise of spring. No matter what, even if it took one hundred years, I would become a good painter.

CHAPTER NINETEEN

Among the Masters

In New York in the mid-fifties, I explored two separate realms within the "art scene," as the city's art world was referred to with a note of rapture by the initiated. One realm revolved around the graduate classes at Hunter College and my friendship with Robert Motherwell. When he married the painter Helen Frankenthaler, Henry and I exchanged an occasional dinner with the Motherwells. That Helen took notice of my paintings hanging on the green walls at Gramercy Park vaguely irritated Motherwell. For him, until I started publishing books, I was solely a young Frenchwoman with amorphous artistic aspirations: he wanted to hear nothing at all about my Russian background. Only my French education met with his approval.

Once in a very great while Motherwell invited me to come with him to some ceremonial event involving museum curators or visiting foreign dignitaries—this was how I met Alfred Barr, with whom I would one day have a formal and yet warmhearted relationship—a relationship based in part on my Russian roots.

One evening Motherwell asked me to go out to dinner with him and the French painter Pierre Soulages. Motherwell's French was not fluent; I was there to facilitate exchanges between the two artists. They were in guarded agreement with each other in matters of artistic creed. They discussed the caves of Lascaux, newly opened to the public, which both men had recently visited. Motherwell described them so eloquently that I could almost see the charging bison, the deer—here would be yet another reason to go back to France for a visit. As they spoke, tactfully yet forcefully, each painter sought to assert his position as the leading abstractionist in his country. They were in complete agreement on the subject of Joan Miro, acclaimed by both artists as the supreme master of international abstraction.

The key to the other realm I was discovering in the New York art world was given to me by Fay Lansner, a painter a bit older than I. Her husband, Kermit Lansner, had been a professor of philosophy at Kenyon College. The Lansners had lived in Europe for several years. Then Kermit became an editor at *Art News*.

I felt at home with Fay, with her joyous paintings of flowers and fruit and of massive female figures. Fay's and Kermit's apartment in a brownstone on Riverside Drive, with its tree-framed view of the Hudson River, had a Mediterranean brightness.

More and more often, after decades of dependence on French art, American painters and the critics who promoted them were denouncing vociferously French influences—the allegedly facile, pastry-sweet Impressionist ones. But Fay, though she had studied with the celebrated German-born Abstract Expressionist Hans Hofmann, could not do this even if she had wanted to: the pictures of Matisse and Picasso, French provincial fabrics and wallpapers, the opulent vegetables she knew how to choose in Manhattan's Greek markets were too much to her liking. I took pleasure in Fay's appreciation of those things that reminded me of my former life.

Fay had studied in France, with André Lhote and then with Léger. She was a member of a cooperative gallery on Central Park South, the Hansa Gallery, which was more eclectic than most galleries, its members younger, more individualistic—and more talented.

Occasionally I posed for Fay. I sat in profile, draped in a blue paisley shawl. While she painted, Fay told me about Hans Hofmann's push-pull theories of color and about Kandinsky's writings on art. If I pressed her, she would recount her childhood in Philadelphia among intellectuals of Russian-Jewish descent. Before the Revolution, in Odessa when she was a young girl, her mother had belonged to the Socialist Revolutionary Party, the SRs, my mother's family's political party. It turned out that Fay and I had a connection beyond our shared fondness for the sensuousness of French art.

Fay was a beautiful, dark-eyed woman with great masses of shiny black hair and a giving, motherly disposition. I loved both her warmth and the singlemindedness of her involvement with her work. Very much at home in New York, Fay knew the best greengrocers below Forty-second Street and the discount shops where one could buy elegant cocktail dresses for almost no money. As a result of her years in Hans Hofmann's studio, she was acquainted with everyone in the art world. Tom Hess, the new editor in chief of *Art News*, was Kermit's close friend.

After a time, Kermit left *Art News* to become editor in chief of *Newsweek*. The Lansners were invited to all the openings and to the parties that were given afterward. More often than not, Kermit, like Henry, preferred to stay home after dinner and work. Fay would ask me to go out with her instead.

The painters' parties of the fifties were held on distant, lower Manhattan streets, deserted at night. Although the city was quite safe in those years—as far as I remember one could, at any hour of the day or night, go by subway anywhere one wished—Fay and I did look after each other on our outings downtown. On her way home in a taxi, Fay might drop me back at 10 Gramercy Park.

Early on in the evening, if we left from Fay's house after a supper she had thrown together with lavish insouciance—Fay was a marvelous natural cook—we would discuss the drawings of Matisse while she put the finishing touches to her costume, choosing a necklace, putting on eye makeup with utmost concentration, as if she were going to pose for Matisse himself. There was a luxuriousness about Fay that was a fine prelude to a party. She was my first American woman friend and remains one of the closest—her passion for painting undiminished.

Thanks to her, with no apprenticeship or seniority whatever on the fiercely competitive New York art scene, I found myself at gatherings where the best-known painters of the time held forth, those whose works, like Motherwell's, were beginning to be sought by the Museum of Modern Art and by the important collectors of the day. Jackson Pollock, Franz Kline, David Smith, Willem De

Kooning, Philip Guston, Ad Reinehardt came to the parties to which
the Lansners were asked. Unassuming, dressed in workmen's
clothes—blue jeans and dark corduroy jackets—each in his own
way was charismatic. They were revered as mythical heroes by a
younger generation of painters, Fay's contemporaries who had studied not long before in Hans Hofmann's Eighth Street studio.

There were several women among these younger painters—Nell
Blaine, Helen Frankenthaler, Joan Mitchell, Jane Frielicher, Grace
Hartigan, and Jane Wilson, who was also a member of the Hansa
Gallery. Regardless of what is said on the subject today, in the fifties
in New York these young women were not discriminated against as
artists if they were talented and especially if they had been students
of Hofmann's. To be recognized they had to be tough; the New
York art world was tough. Fay was an exception: she was not tough.
Moreover, despite her schooling she painted recognizable nudes and
bouquets and was openly admiring of other people's gifts. This was
exceptional in a circle of artists where cliquishness prevailed, exacerbated perhaps in some by the lack of social status of the turn of-
the-century immigrants who had been their grandfathers. As a rule
the New York art scene was in these years independent of old
American cultural institutions. Outsiders were discouraged through
an aggressive haughtiness often verging on rudeness.

As far as the legacy of the older generation of Abstract Expressionists was concerned, Motherwell put it this way in his class,
weariness coming over his face like a mask—a mask which made it
awkward to ask him to elaborate on his statement. "I think that my
colleagues and I have made it clear once and for all: Nowadays the
only subject matter worthy of a painter is his innermost self." An
increasing number of New Yorkers, including Motherwell, were re-
sorting to Freudian analysis, but it remained the prerogative of the
rich until other, less costly psychotherapies became available in the
United States.

For the average art student the question remained: How does one
fathom one's innermost self? How does one translate it in paint?
Motherwell would not say. Evidently he and his contemporaries
knew techniques that enabled them to accomplish this successfully,
but in practice their secrets remained all too well guarded. With a
few exceptions American art today exists mostly as elaborate replays

of old modernist clichés. This loss of artistic heritage would not become evident for a long time: In the mid-fifties American art was ebullient, its future full of promise.

It is said now that mercantile interests and fear of Communism had combined forces to displace Paris in favor of New York as the world art center. American assertiveness was elemental. A taste for European and Japanese artistic refinements was brought back home by war veterans who were keenly aware of their status as victors in the conflict. And the revelation of the immensity of Stalin's crimes had made old quarrels within the American Left less strident. Most people of goodwill, however grudgingly, recognized the enormity of the Soviet disaster. As far as I know, only the obstinate Lillian Hellman remained unwilling to alter her convictions concerning Stalin.

To converse with a celebrated Abstract Expressionist at a gallery opening, to sit afterward at his table in the Cedar Street Tavern on University Place—these were prodigious events in a younger painter's life. What if the key to tomorrow's great art were to be revealed in the course of an evening downtown? But the Abstract Expressionist painting techniques remained elusive beyond a certain automatism inspired by the late works of Monet; by Edvard Munch, whose show at the Museum of Modern Art had recently been a revelation; and by the endearing Zen monks eulogized by Allan Watts.

Without exception, the older painters were fond of Fay and made her very much welcome among them. However, they discussed art, and cryptically at that, only with their own peers. They formed a close-knit, comradly group. Conversations in the Cedar Street Tavern, where the generations mingled, remained casual. Pollock wanted to know whether Fay and her husband might soon be visiting the Springs on Long Island where he now lived—he hoped Kermit would write about his new work in *Art News*. If he was drunk he glowered and said nothing. Rothko smiled upon seeing Fay in a crowd and gave her an affectionate hug.

Whenever I was in the company of the Abstract Expressionist masters, I spoke as little as possible. If asked directly what I did, I would say that I was a schoolteacher. It was out of the question to admit to being an intruder—a lowly and yet potentially threatening art student. The one time I said I was a ballet dancer resulted in an unwelcome proposition. Though no longer needed as models, evidently dancers were still assumed to be sexually available.

I listened, and I studied the faces. The rewards of a life spent in working-class New York at the center of a dynamic immigrant culture were there to see. Franz Kline and Jackson Pollock looked like longshoremen, strong and aggressive. Guston had the dark, languorous eyes of a Persian prince and sounded passionate and yet soft-spoken. De Kooning sparkled with childlike humor. Rothko resembled the old socialists who came to my parents' apartment when I was a child.

He was a retiring middle-aged man. Like my parents' beloved friend Isaac Babel, Rothko had "spectacles on his nose and autumn in his heart." In his pictures, washes of translucent colors were like shades drawn over some event deliberately hidden from the viewer's sight. Before they became dark and threatening, these pictures were wondrously pleasing, painted with an unusual sensitivity to the glowing surfaces they exhibited to the world.

One evening, emboldened by what I regarded as my insight into Rothko's art, I asked him about his background—was it not something frightening out of his childhood—a scene of devastation, a pogrom perhaps—that was lurking behind the gorgeous screens in his pictures? One of the things I loved about New York was that it was acceptable to ask a stranger about his or her childhood wherever one went—in France asking such questions of strangers would have been considered inappropriate.

When I asked Rothko this question it was past midnight in one of Fay's former schoolmates', Larry Rivers, studio on lower Fourth Avenue, which was then the Ukrainian and Gypsy part of town. Rothko replied in a friendly manner that, indeed, he had been born in Russia and had witnessed his share of horrible events there. With him as with Fay I had invisible roots in common Old World socialist roots, which helped me lose my shyness whenever we conversed.

Rothko knew the works of my grandfather Leonid Andreyev. He remembered *The Seven Who Were Hanged*, the intricacies of Andreyev's friendship with Gorky, their common stand against anti-Semitism, and Andreyev's denunciation of capital punishment. In Larry

Rivers's studio he seemed an exile, like Chagall in his plush Ile de la Cité apartment—there the émigré artist with the heavy Russian accent appeared never to have left his beloved Vitebsk, even as the quays of the Seine stretched languorously below his windows.

I remember being struck by the generosity of spirit with which Americans such as Fay and Rothko regarded things Russian, not identifying the people and the writers with the government that had driven their grandparents into exile. Late at night, for hours, Harold Rosenberg, Philip Rhav, and Rothko discussed Dostoyevsky and Tolstoy. I remember Rothko speaking about Tolstoy's last days, the flight to Astapovo, the funeral train ride. Tolstoy in old age fascinated Rothko. The Russian's predicament reflected his growing inner despair, the void looming behind the shimmering surface of his pictures.

CHAPTER TWENTY

Downtown

Through Fay Lansner I became acquainted with some of her fellow students from Hans Hofmann's studio, the master now taught only in Provincetown. As a rule, they were painters a very few years older than I—Woolf Khan, Robert Goodenough, Paul Resika, Jane Wilson. Then in their early thirties, they were the artists who were seeking recognition as the "Second Generation of New York Expressionists." All were talented. The competitiveness among them was relentless. They seemed to lack that warm complicity that linked the older artists to each other. For the first time in my life I could observe firsthand the workings of undisguised ambition.

I had been brought up to believe that the making of art was a spiritual endeavor, that early recognition had little to do with it. Larionov and Gontcharova, the Russian artists whom we knew in Paris, kept some of their early works under a couch, a permanent, seemingly acceptable state of affairs. They pulled these out on occasion to show them to admirers who came to tea in their studio. Early on in Le Plessis, Leonid Andreyev's charcoal study after Goya's *Devils Cutting Their Nails* had been kept under my parents' bed.

But here in New York the younger artists were yearning for exposure, they came together to discuss galleries and collectors. Of course there was also friendship and joking and drinking, and often dancing. Soon there would be drugs sweeping in from Harlem. The music was that of Miles Davis's records with a Charlie Parker tune

suddenly taking over and holding everyone in its power. Miles Davis's trumpet was a lone angry voice that still suggested the existence
of a community. The social fragmentation that rock and roll would
herald had not yet taken place.

Guests danced and drank relentlessly, and they wheeled and deal-
ed. No one ever seemed to be totally lost in conversation or drink
or love. There were few overt flirtations. To a Parisian this was
remarkable. After the war in Paris we had lived with the electrifying
myth of *"Amour Fou,"* first formulated by the Surrealists and then
glorified by Picasso. *Amour Fou* was irrepressible. It gave erotic over-
tones to any encounter with the opposite sex, no matter how banal.
But there was little of it in New York: Fay and I remained quite
safe wherever we went together or separately. Of course, that we
were married was understood. Less prestigious than Kermit's position at *Newsweek*, Henry's as an editor at Knopf nonetheless inspired
a measure of respect whenever it was mentioned at New York parties.

No matter how crowded the party, the painters of New York
were glancing at the door, looking for gallery owners and art dealers
from uptown who had been invited and might—or might not—be
coming downtown. Magazine writers and critics were eagerly
awaited. Whenever Clement Greenberg or Harold Rosenberg walked
in, guests would fall silent and drift into a circle that would steadily
grow.

Betty Parsons was one of the gallery owners who often did come
downtown. She wore hand-loomed clothes, like Georgia O'Keeffe's
in her portraits, and heavy, whimsical jewelry designed by Alexander
Calder, who was living in France then. Her eyes were light blue,
like ice, and her manner was glacial as well. For a young artist to
be noticed by her, was the difference between being and nonbeing.

A lull would settle upon a party whenever Johnny Mayers of the
Tibor de Nagy Gallery walked in, usually quite late in the evening.
Johnny Mayers was a large red-haired man who moved with jerky
movements and had a very loud, raucous laugh. He went around
with an entourage of handsome young male artists. Most striking
among them was dark-eyed, sharp-featured Larry Rivers, one of the
very few painters of his generation who openly challenged the strictures of the abstract ethic. His monumental naturalistic nudes of his

mother-in-law, Birdie, were exhibited at the Museum of Modern Art, scandalizing New York's recent converts to abstraction. Rivers was a jazz musician as well as a painter and was said to be using heroin.

Larry Rivers painted recognizable people and objects. His *George Washington Crossing the Delaware*, a sketchily painted, outsize historical scene had been recently purchased by the Museum of Modern Art. Whenever Larry was not in the company of Johnny Mayers, he had his own entourage of young men that included the poet Frank O'Hara, who worked at the Museum of Modern Art.

Fay introduced me to O'Hara one evening. O'Hara had a charming intensity and was obviously beloved by his peers, men and women. He was anxious to discuss Russian poetry—he especially admired Mayakovsky. He had recently read what is to this day one of my favorite books, Boris Pasternak's *Safe Conduct*, first published in English in the late forties.

I knew bits of *Safe Conduct* by heart, windows onto my family's unattainable Russia. Its modernistic style brought people and objects into focus with a Cubist's sharpness. "Years went by and it was winter out of doors. The street was foreshortened by at least a third with twilight and with furs. The cubes of carriages and lanterns sped along it silently." But Frank O'Hara preferred Mayakovsky to Pasternak. "What grandeur, the sweeping lines are fabulous. You know of course that Mayakovsky was inspired by Walt Whitman."

There was among Larry's friends a mustachioed young man named Howard Kanowitz, with whom I struck an acquaintanceship. Unlike the other painters who affected a forbidding manner with a stranger, Kanowitz was eager to share his experiences and to talk—about his childhood in working-class New England, in Fall River, and about New York, which he loved with the passion of a recent arrival from the provinces. In addition to being a painter he was a jazz musician like Rivers, and he knew where the best jazz could be heard on any given night in New York. He was ready to take me to the right parties to hear it, but I never went, I did not want to stray away from Fay's protective presence.

Still I shared in the rapture of that newborn freedom that was sweeping through New York. I knew that black Americans being included as equals was a novelty. I occasionally went to the Metropolitan Museum with an exceptionally gifted black painter called Bob Thompson. He was in his early twenties and belonged to that other, jazz-oriented art world that I did not wish to enter. It was menacing, in it people used drugs—not only marijuana, but heroin, or even a new, amazing discovery called LSD, which was also coming into the New York literary milieu through Timothy Leary, a teacher of philosophy at Harvard. I knew that drugs were dangerous. They had been widely used in the Montparnasse Bohemia in my parents' youth. My father's close friend, the Russian émigré poet, Boris Poplavsky had died of an overdose in the thirties. Certain writers we knew, such as Harold Humes and Terry Southern, were beginning to use drugs freely.

Years before Soho became a separate avant-garde kingdom, the New York painters' studios were located just below Fourteenth Street, in old commercial buildings left in disuse for decades. Many had once been factories, others had housed elegant, turn-of-the-century shops. They still had tall windows framed by carved, decaying moldings and very high ceilings. In order to be able to afford the rent, the artists were often forced to share space, two or three to a loft. They whitewashed the peeling walls and tacked their canvases on them. The house paints they used dripped on the floor and formed ridges. Or else, like Pollock and Helen Frankenthaler, they painted as they moved around expanses of canvas laid out flat on the floor.

The lofts' furnishings were minimal, a bed in a corner, a chair or two, a table, a washstand, and a toilet haphazardly installed behind a makeshift partition. The spaces left for work were immense, as were the pictures.

Ostensibly, under law, New York lofts could not be used as residences, but artists lived in them, anyway, striking deals with the housing inspectors who came by periodically. Every week, one of the artists would throw an all-night party, one that would not have been tolerated elsewhere in the city. Such parties, usually with live jazz, would be given in a residential section of town only when someone was ready to move away and no longer cared about his neighbors' goodwill.

After a gallery opening, one of the New York painters would invite everyone from the art scene to the run-down commercial loft where he lived and worked. Around nine o'clock there would be candles burning throughout in the studio, and open bottles of red wine and clusters of people in blue jeans and in beautiful Bohemian-looking costumes created out of leotards and long black skirts, fringed shawls, and Mexican silver jewelry.

Though Fay introduced me to her friends in the most flattering manner, often even praising my work to them, it took all my courage to follow her as she boldly plunged into the dense, forbidding crowds. I was sustained by my curiosity. I wanted to see at close range the striking faces and the costumes, trying to link these in my mind with the canvases hanging in full light on gallery walls or lurking in the dim recesses of the artists' lofts. Had I not recently found a key to the art of Rothko, a secretive man who was trying to come to terms with the golden country that was beginning to acclaim his gifts? I was looking for recognitions in the shadowy lofts of lower Manhattan.

These however would usually turn out to be literary, and Russian at that. As for the pictures, all too often to me they looked bland—lifeless overlapping surfaces stretching on and on. Or else violent swirls of color or dead black surfaces like Ad Reinhardt's. I stared at these without recognition of any sort, and I felt ashamed of my lack of responsiveness, for they were universally admired, and their creator and his wife and daughter were a friendly, warmhearted family. The Reinhardts were neighbors who lived in the vicinity of Gramercy Park.

Throughout the decade we spent in New York, the art scene was forever shifting and its tempo accelerating. More and more young artists from all over the country came there every year. In them I recognized the sense of awakening I had felt as I walked the twilight streets of the thirteenth arrondissement on my way to meet Henry on rue de Seine: snatches of Piaf's songs had told me then that love was somewhere nearby, in the heart of old Paris. Now Miles Davis was speaking about the future of the New World, but in a voice filled with nostalgia. Or was it perhaps the past that he was cele-brating?

Yet, a new Bohemian sensibility was being born in America. The initiated were giddy, they were possessed with a frenzy of wanting not to miss anything that might be *new*. In fact, it was drugs that were new.

They were erupting onto the New York art scene on a huge scale. The visible world was becoming ever less important to artists, whereas drug-induced transcendental states of mind, not artichokes, served as artistic subject matter.

Still, self-centered as they were, the aspiring young artists of New York were earnest. They not only yearned to be famous, they also wanted to be good artists. They believed that their art, though done in the prevalent Abstract Expressionist mode, had also to be original. One's power of self-renewal was an obsession, a favorite subject of conversation. Newness in art was imperative, a canon legitimized by Alfred Barr, the apprentice sorcerer of American modernism who had made it the rule of acceptance into the sanctuary of the Museum of Modern Art.

With a personality shaped by the best of European avant-garde before the war, Barr was the ultimate judge in America of what was really new. By this time pop art was beginning to displace Abstract Expressionism. I remember Barr's barely disguised dismay at a party at the Sculls' apartment on the Upper East Side. The Sculls, owners of a taxicab fleet, were the leading collectors of pop. The vast, luxurious apartment was filled with Rosenquists and Oldenburgs. There were ceramic hamburgers scattered all over the place and the bathroom fixtures were gilded, as was Ethel Scull herself, in a tight-fitting gold lamé dress. The white wall-to-wall carpeting was so thick that my pumps kept sinking into it. Barr spoke about his stay in Moscow in 1928. Had anyone he had admired there survived Stalin's terror? No one knew for sure.

But it was for American art that Alfred Barr was grieving. He had hoped for a better future than the ghastly looking ceramic hamburgers and the vegetables scattered around us. Yet pop proved enduring, the dominant international style that reigns today in all its banality disguised as novelty. One by one, museums with an eclectic approach to art collecting are "restructured" so as to favor dubious innovations. Most recently, this kind of curatorial change of guard happened at the Museum of Fine Arts in Boston.

For the notion that painting might thrive on deepening and expanding existing traditions rather than destroying them died in New York in the fifties. Within his life span an artist was expected to change continuously—that was the consecrated expression. Accord-

ing to this perception, from his early impressionistic studies Matisse
had progressed to the abstract *papiers decoupés* of his last years. Monet
had gone on to ever looser forms in his *Nymphéas*; the fact that his
vision had become blurred with age was not considered: his evolu-
tion was seen as a triumphant artistic march toward ultimate abstraction. Bonnard, who had not changed dramatically his style from
year to year, was not considered important, his work "did not
count."

I remember Philip Guston at one of his openings at the Stable
Gallery on Sixth Avenue, established in a remodeled stable, a space
that reminded one that New York, ever evolving like the works of
its artists, had only recently been a traditional Victorian city. Guston's nonfigurative paintings were heavenly looking, pink and green
sunsets, sweeter than even Monet's celebrated *Impressions* now at the
Marmottan Museum in Paris. Like Guston's physique, they were
outrageously beautiful, an aspect of his art that he set out to destroy
deliberately in his later works.

Guston's decision to return to a powerfully grotesque figuration
was unpopular at first but would win him enormous posthumous
acclaim. However, this would not happen for years—when it did,
his raw, Eastern European immigrant roots were revealed with un-
precedented strength. He had the courage to explore them rather
than pull shades, however beautiful, over his grim visions. Like
Rothko he too killed himself, but he did it slowly, through alcohol
as did so many of his brilliant American contemporaries.

Back in the mid-fifties, however, Guston's pictures looked like
variations on late Monets, but without a recognizable subject matter.
At that time these, and David Smith's sculptures, were Motherwell's
favorite contemporary American artworks. His praise of Guston was
ecstatic.

At his party, speaking in a grave, low-keyed voice, Guston said
to Fay that only *truth* mattered in painting and that it was achieved
when each and every part of a picture was imbued with a sense of
the infinite. The next day, when I quoted this statement to my father
who had studied art history at the University of Berlin in the twenties, he said matter-of-factly that this had once been John Ruskin's
conception of art, and before him, Kant's. But this perspective on
Abstract Expressionism did not satisfy me. A product of French

education, I looked for clear formulations. Would easel painting eventually disappear, as Henry sometimes said? How was I to proceed beyond the nature-inspired still lifes and portraits and cityscapes that I painted every day in our living room on Gramercy Park?

I could have gone to Columbia University to study with the art historian Meyer Shapiro. I had heard him lecture on Cézanne at the New School. I knew that he was supremely intelligent and knowledgeable and collected works by the best young figurative artists, notably those of Bob Thompson, the most original among them. Not scholarly minded just then, I preferred to look for clues about the future of painting and my own in museums, and especially in my contemporaries' studios as I wandered through their cavernous lofts while they drank and danced to the music of Miles Davis.

A childhood spent in France during the German occupation made it easy enough for me to remain inconspicuous. Yet when someone looked approachable, like Rothko, all I had to do was ask this person about his or her background. Then I'd hear prodigious stories about how a new, intoxicating America had come into being— stories of immigrant life; of survival during the Depression; of the huge hope that Franklin Roosevelt had given Americans, a hope that still inspired many whom one met in New York in those years.

This new America fascinated me—it was right there before me to be discovered. The literary side of it, accessible to me through Henry's work in publishing, was heady yet intelligible and challenging. We had friendships with James Baldwin, William Styron, Terry Southern, Philip Roth, Mary Lee Settle, with the sparkling, cantankerous Norman Mailer, and with Robert Penn Warren and his wife, Eleanor Clark. Some of these writers and their families became family friends. But the painters populating the New York art world, with its complex plays of power, were mine alone to try to fathom and perhaps to join.

My investigations of the artists' studios exhausted me quickly. After an hour or two I would want to get out, to walk the cool dark streets and put my thoughts in order. In New York at night the gigantic straight perspectives, the gloom of an urban landscape that was becoming ever more deserted, drew me in. Only rarely did I have to cross the street to avoid a drunken man staggering along the sidewalk. Here in downtown Manhattan people from all over Europe had once been forced to mix and live together and give up their past. To survive they had had to will themselves into a state of collective amnesia. Now their children had moved to grander neighborhoods, yet something of their parents' lives could be sensed behind the empty tenement facades, the boarded up warehouses whose spirit Edward Hopper, one of America's great artists who was all but ignored in the fifties, has captured for all time.

Having said good-night to Fay, I walked back uptown to Gramercy Park, where Henry would be working on his first book late into the night. One hot spring night I came upon Little Italy, a sudden island of Italian music and lantern-lit outdoor dancing. Despite the unlikely backdrop of glum brownstones it felt like the fiesta in Collioure on that town's Saint's Day in the heat of summer, in what seemed a lifetime away. I stood there aching for France, for the south of France. That was where I wanted to go.

But soon my life took an unexpected turn. Russia claimed me, it was to Russia that I went instead. I never gave up France, nor did I stop painting. To this day I love painting more than anything, yet sometime in the mid-sixties, little by little, I lost the self-induced, obsessive conviction that painting was life's ultimate value. I don't think that it was entirely a matter of talent: I lacked the drive needed to try to forge a visible artistic career for myself. My good fortune is that in California, where we now live, there has been a tradition of "painterly" painting since the fifties. Led by artists such as Richard Diebenkorn and Wayne Tibaud, stemming from masters I especially admire, notably Matisse and Bonnard, it is alive to this day, and I feel I belong to it.

As for France, Henry and I symbolically made it our own by restoring a small house in Provence that we had bought as a ruin in 1962, and where I now have a painting studio. On the way through Paris I often visit Olivier Pagès and his wife. France is for me a country of the heart.

One of three.

PART III

Russia

CHAPTER TWENTY-ONE

Poetry and Politics

A new path opened itself to me—writing. In the Khrushchev era of the late fifties, an exploration of Russia's recent history, however partial, opened a brighter future not only to that country, but also to the people to whom I had belonged from birth, the scattered tribe of Russian émigrés. During this time I began reporting on the newly emerging Russia; this proved an absorbing, long-term endeavor. My Russian career started through New York friends who were writers. Somewhat inadvertently I was given an assignment by the *Paris Review* to travel to Russia and interview Boris Pasternak, who was awarded the Nobel Prize in 1958 for his novel *Doctor Zhivago*.

My journey to Moscow in the winter of 1959–60 was the beginning of a new life, a slow acquaintance with my parents' country that engages me to this day. It was a personal commitment that Henry wholeheartedly supported. I never joined any kind of organization. Even now my nonpartisanship seems to serve a good cause, helping scale the mountain of misunderstandings that rise between the USA and Russia. I like to think that over the years my extremely circumspect reporting about Russian affairs might have contributed in some infinitesimal degree to the emergence of glasnost.

My early trips to Russia took me back to what had been at the core of my life until I left home for Bard College in 1949—poetry. Then it had been Russian poetry, which was my father's all-consuming passion. Our family's friendship with Marina Tsvetayeva had continued until 1939, when she returned to Russia. There she found herself at the center of a Soviet secret police snake pit whose horror has become fully known only recently. There she committed suicide in the provincial town of Elabuga, an event that has become the stuff of legend in Russia, the kind of legend that people tell to terrify one another. She herself was the author in the twenties of a chilling version in verse of the Dracula legend, *Molodetz*. When I was a child on the island of Oléron during the war years, we read and reread this fabulous long poem, unaware of the fact that just then Marina Tsvetayeva was dying in circumstances far grimmer than anything she could have imagined.

Now that I was beginning to write in English, English and American poetry became part of my life also. This happened as a result of that initial trip in 1959, a momentous adventure, a return to a homeland I had never seen. I recorded this in a memoir published by Random House in 1963, *Voices in the Snow*. It was subsequently published in France and then circulated in typescript passed from hand to hand—*samizdat*—in the Soviet Union in the sixties and seventies. In the United States it was well received by the literary establishment.

My meetings with Pasternak and the friendships I formed with my contemporaries, the young poets of Moscow—Bulat Okudzhava, Bella Ahmadulina, Andrey Voznesensky, Yevgueny Yevtushenko—led in turn to encounters with American poets who at that time were intrigued by their counterparts in Russia. By the mid-sixties, poetry, both Russian and English, swept into my life like a tide.

Right after *Voices in the Snow* was published, Joe Fox, a friend and editor at Random House, had given me a small advance to create a bilingual anthology of contemporary Russian poetry. I worked on *Poets on Street Corners* for several years. At a time when Pasternak, Mandelstam, and Tsvetayeva were forbidden in the Soviet Union, I collected their poems in manuscript and asked several American poets to adapt them freely, using my literal translations as a basis for poetic renditions in English.

Imitations. The term had been used by the American poet Robert Lowell in 1958, in his collection by this name, one which he then revised repeatedly. In a 1963 edition, which he had given me, he wrote: "To Olga with sympathy and admiration. I hope the free translations of Pasternak I have made here will show my reverence. Robert Lowell." In his inscription, "sympathy" refers to my plight as an émigrée: Lowell had a poet's visceral compassion for those who have lost their country, in my case a country I had only recently discovered at first hand. "It makes me sad: You can't be but far from Russia," he would say. In his perception, I had been exiled both from the French and the Russian languages, and he tried to make me welcome to his own tongue.

On occasion Lowell took me to poetry readings. I remember one, of Yeats's poems at Columbia University, and one given by Eliot at the 92nd Street Y. He would share whatever he was reading at a given time—Flannery O'Connor, Malcolm Lowery, Charlotte Steed's *Man Who Loved Children*. He recited to me a great deal of his own verse as it was written and rewritten.

His mood swings caused Lowell to rework his poems endlessly. This he did regularly with his students in class. One of them, Philip Levine, at Iowa, objected to this invasion by Lowell's poetry of hours that should have been focused solely on pupils work. Not a student myself, I was thrilled. I was a well-trained listener. My father had tried his poems on my mother and myself, always. And many of the poems on which Lowell worked in the early sixties were magnificent.

I believe that his inscription in *Imitations*, "admiration" refers to my persistence in continuing to paint in the face of the fashionable American art of the day. Robert Lowell loved and understood painting. He had an all-consuming interest in early American art. Until he left for Ireland in the early seventies, visits to museums in New York in his company were a wondrous routine whenever I came into town from Connecticut, where we lived from 1965 to 1977. In those years, Henry and I sometimes stayed overnight in the small studio that Robert Lowell and his wife Elizabeth Hardwick owned at 15 West Sixty-seventh Street, on the top floor of the building that housed their duplex apartment near Central Park.

As I started to write professionally, Henry's steady support was essential. It helped me find a voice of my own, a first-person narrative suited to the stories I wanted to tell. My written English was only beginning to develop. Henry, who had resigned from publishing to become a full-time novelist, edited my articles. I traveled to Russia as a journalist in 1960, 1962, 1965, and twice in 1967. I wrote dozens of articles and four books on contemporary Russian subjects. Eventually Henry and I joined forces on behalf of Russian dissenters. In the early seventies, Henry was elected president of American PEN and was especially active in organizing its Freedom to Write committee, which publicized the repressions to which writers were subjected in the USSR.

Planning my time as best I could, I was able to continue to paint. To be asked to exhibit at the distinguished Katia Granoff Gallery on quai de Conti in Paris was an undreamed of breakthrough. My brother's first wife, Judith Andreyev, a talented musician, liked my work. Tirelessly she helped me organize my transatlantic exhibits—Sasha had settled in Paris with his family. Later Judith and Gloria Loomis, a close friend who would become my literary agent, worked hard on the English in *Voices in the Snow*, which Robert Loomis patiently edited. Bob taught me "not to pontificate," even when I touched on momentous Russian subjects.

My French friends came to my shows, including Aline and Olivier Pagès and Jean-Pierre: their anti-American feelings had subsided. These shows gave me the impetus to persevere, as did my friendship with a true lover of painting, the Austrian photographer Inge Morath, with whom I worked on several books of pictures and texts on Russian themes. Translating Dostoyevsky's *Idiot* for the New American Library together with Henry was a labor of love for us both and proved also an invaluable literary apprenticeship. Later on we translated together Alexander Solzhenitzyn's *First Circle* and two of the three volumes of *Gulag Archipelago*.

Over the years Henry wrote several successful novels—two light-hearted ones on Russian and San Francisco motifs, respectively. These were followed by three historical novels, using his fascination with the darker side of American history. One of them, *Voyage to the First of December*, kept us financially secure for a number of years. Later we collaborated on the recently published *The Idealists*, about the Russian Revolution, which combined Henry's novelistic skills and my knowledge of things Russian.

I owe my friendship with Robert Lowell to Boris Pasternak. It was as if upon Pasternak's death in May 1960, he had brought us together as an afterthought. In January of that year in Peredelkino, still in good health, Pasternak had given me a lengthy interview on the theme of "Writers at Work." Some months later, when it was published in the *Paris Review*, at Lowell's request a mutual acquaintance introduced us. The text, reprinted in the magazine *Encounter*, had caught Lowell's attention.

Three years before that, *Doctor Zhivago* had caused a sensation in the West. For the first time since Stalin's death the world was reminded that a rich, modernistic literature existed in Russia despite the persecutions inflicted on those artists who dared challenge the Communist ideology, however obliquely. Pasternak's fate at the hands of the authorities, which had harassed him and forced him to give up his Nobel Prize and most probably hastened his end, had aroused Western public opinion.

For despite the so-called thaw following Khrushchev's 1956 revelations about Stalin's crimes, the Soviet government remained relentless in its efforts to maintain absolute control over Russian cultural life. In 1961 American intellectuals were outraged by the arrest of Pasternak's lover, Olga Ivinskaya. Shortly after the poet's death she had been seized by the Secret Police for receiving Western currency from the Italian publisher of *Doctor Zhivago*. Petitions on her behalf circulated in New York. Intellectuals from a wide spectrum of political opinions were signing them—it was before the better known among them were showered with invitations to the USSR issued by the KGB-controlled Moscow Writers Union. This would be part of a disinformation campaign that lasted more than twenty years.

But protests by Westerners had little, if any, effect on the Soviet Union's internal policies against dissenting writers and intellectuals. Olga Ivinskaya and her daughter Irina served out their terms in labor camp. *Doctor Zhivago* would be published in Russia only in 1989, after the Soviet state's collapse.

In retrospect one can suppose that, had the authorities not taken from the beginning such an uncompromising stand about this highly poetic, esoteric novel, had they allowed it to come out in a censored version, the course of Soviet history might have been different. The subject of a book that did not directly question the legitimacy of Communist rule, they themselves created a never-ending scandal, a precedent upon which they were forced to act until the end. As time passed, the *Zhivago* affair exacerbated the zeal of party functionaries. It prepared the ground for an escalation of challenges to Soviet power, culminating with the publication in the West of Alexander Solzhenitsyn's *Gulag Archipelago*.

But in New York in 1961 Robert Lowell, like many others including myself, was persuaded that Olga Ivinskaya's release could be secured through a show of public indignation, a campaign of protests by influential Westerners. Active in this campaign were Lowell's friends connected with *Encounter* magazine, including the poet Stephen Spender and the musician Nicholas Nabokov. However, I discovered that Lowell involved himself in a very personal way with the Russian poet's legacy. He identified with Pasternak to an unusual degree; he was possessed by an obsessive, chivalrous concern for Ivinskaya and her daughter. It was moving and somewhat disconcerting until one realized that Lowell, like Pasternak, had extramarital affairs, and took especially to heart the fate of a woman persecuted because of an illicit liaison.

I remember vividly my first encounter with Lowell on a brilliant midspring day. I remember the sunshine, the sea-borne smells of Manhattan in warm weather. There were three of us. A mutual friend, Robert Silvers, took us to lunch on Third Avenue in midtown, to Le Moal, which was popular with writers in those years. Although it was close to the bar frequented by Motherwell after his evening classes, Le Moal was as removed from that bar's working class Irishness as it was from the closely watched, claustrophobic cafés where I had often had to meet my Russian friends in Moscow. Le Moal was French. One could order ray in black butter there, and calf brains with capers, and speak as freely as one wanted.

And indeed Lowell's words flowed wildly. I knew nothing of the manic depression that would erupt within him, as often as twice a year. Until we met the Lowells, Henry and I knew few American poets personally, although at Knopf Henry had edited one of W. S. Merwin's early collections. We had read some of Lowell's majestic early poems, notably "The Quaker Cemetery at Madeket"; we had a warm friendship with Harry Ford who was both a brilliant book designer and the poetry editor at Knopf. However as a rule then as today, poets lived in the world of academe, which was not yet the case with novelists and editors. In those years Robert Lowell's frequent mental breakdowns were seldom discussed in public. The times were less given to confession, less invasive of privacy, though Lowell himself greatly contributed to establishing a confessional mode in literature. In any case, these episodes, had they been publicized, would have thrown a shadow on the poet's considerable reputation as a teacher and academic lecturer.

The subjects he touched upon that day dealt for the most part with Russia. He spoke of his admiration of *Doctor Zhivago*. For him and his wife, the critic Elizabeth Hardwick, and their circle of friends, including the long-divorced Mary McCarthy and Edward Wilson, *Doctor Zhivago* served as a yardstick in matters of literary appreciation. They loved the novel despite the distancing effect of an imperfect translation. For Lowell personally, Pasternak's portrait of the poet as healer was seductive though clearly not within his reach.

Lowell's feelings poured forth, the utterances of a manic-depressive individual during a high that would end in turmoil and mental collapse. He told me that his wife was working on a play about the Bolshevik leader Bukharin. He spoke about the Great Purges of the thirties and asked questions about my background as the daughter of a Parisian émigré poet and granddaughter of a Russian socialist defeated by Lenin. He had read stories by Leonid Andreyev, including *The Seven Who were Hanged*, but he knew little of Russian poetry beyond what was published at the time in English and notably the Penguin bilingual volume edited by Dmitry Obolensky, which he had used as a point of departure for some of the poems in *Imitations*. He asked me whether I would be willing to look at his Pasternak renditions, which he wished to bring closer to the originals without altering their integrity in English.

As the luncheon progressed I sensed that Bob Silvers was becoming uncomfortable. Evidently he was aware of Lowell's propensity to plunge into reckless love affairs whenever a manic high was settling in. But I had no idea of this, I was fresh out of Russia where the poets I encountered had taken me in as one of their own because of my family background. I found it natural that Lowell was inviting me to go with him the following week to see Racine's *Andromaque*, presented in New York by the visiting Comédie Française.

The fate of abused women haunted Lowell that day. Later I

discovered that there had been episodes of violence against women early in his life. I myself never witnessed anything of the sort, although I saw him on occasion in disoriented states when he was about to be committed—I visited him on several occasions when he was confined in mental institutions. During that first luncheon he recited his adaptation of Baudelaire's "The Swan." The swan was a mythological bird for Lowell, a symbol upon which he often touched, and again when he and his wife visited in Connecticut some years later. A swan graced a pond near our house. Here is Lowell's rendition of this poem, one of Baudelaire's greatest:

> Andromache, I think of you. Here men
> move on, diminished from those grander years,
> when Racine's tirades scourged our greasy Seine,
> this lying trickle swollen with your tears!

Because of his illness Robert Lowell was not there for *Andromaque*, but I did see the opulent production of the play that had so bored Aline and myself a few years before when we studied it at Marie-Curie. But now André Malraux was presiding over the reviving of French cultural heritage. After the long years when I had been impervious to the grandeur of the French classics, the poetic power of Racine reached me. As a rule my family and my Larcouëst friends favored the subversive French authors, the *poetes maudits*: Beaudelaire, Verlaine, Nerval, Lautreamont, Rimbaud. Henry loved these poets too, when he lived on rue de Seine he had been translating *Une saison en enfer* into English.

A few days after our luncheon, Robert Lowell was hospitalized. But even before that happened, on that first sunny day I realized that beyond his brilliance, his enormous powers of empathy, his literary gifts, Robert Lowell was a profoundly troubled man. That night I dreamed about Gérard de Nerval, the nineteenth-century French poet who had hanged himself in Paris in a fit of insanity. This dream helped me recognize from the beginning the weight imposed by Robert Lowell's illness on those around him. This recognition it made it possible for our friendship to grow and endure.

Some weeks later when Lowell was released from the Riggs Institute in Hartford, Henry and I were invited to the Lowells for dinner. They had recently moved to Sixty-seventh Street in Manhattan from Boston, where the poet would still be teaching part of the time. The other guests that night were Lillian Hellman, with whom we were on distant but cordial terms. Robert Silvers, the mutual friend who had introduced me to Lowell, an intimate of Elizabeth Hardwick's, was there too. The evening was evidently in the nature of a test to determine whether Henry and I might be included within the Lowells' larger circle of acquaintances.

Elizabeth Hardwick, a slight, graceful woman, wore chiffon. She had a marked southern accent and a brilliant critical mind that expressed itself in a fireworks of shimmering literary insights—the conversation was about Melville and about old friends of the Lowells, originally from the South—Robert Penn Warren and especially Randall Jarrell, whose death some months later would devastate Lowell. On that very first evening Elizabeth Hardwick, who became a good friend, must have realized at once that I would be no threat to her husband's precarious mental equilibrium. Leonid Andreyev had evidently been a manic-depressive. Through my father's book about his childhood I had gained an awareness of this affliction, which often affects highly creative individuals. In fact, working on translations was quite therapeutic for Lowell, particularly in his post-manic periods before he was ready to go back to his own writing. I could be useful in this respect, and indeed I was, soon afterward, introducing him to the works of the great Russian poet Osip Mandelstam.

This evening was like many others that Henry and I attended in New York in those years. Those present, excepting the intimidated new arrivals, would be affirming his or her literary status. This was a realm of Pulitzer Prizes, of Broadway plays, and of government-sponsored trips abroad.

As the evening progressed, it became clear to both of us that Lowell and his wife were possessed by a fierce sense of competitiveness, especially with each other. They played roles. Lowell, "Cal," as he was known to his friends, was the Boston aristocratic man of letters. Lizzie was the southerner, the self-made writer with a working-class background who had a special regard for President Roosevelt for all he had done for the underprivileged in America. By comparison with the Lowells, Lillian Hellman, a commanding presence under any circumstance, appeared relaxed. This was a couple of years before Elizabeth Hardwick criticized one of Lillian's plays in the newborn *New York Review of Books*, where she acted as drama critic. This led to an estrangement between Lillian and Elizabeth. As far as I remember, it upset Robert Lowell but he remained loyal to both women.

Indeed, Lowell had a gift for friendships with women, although St. Mark's and Harvard educated as he was, he had numerous lifelong male friends. One was Blair Clark, a retired CBS executive who supported the Lowells with extraordinary devotion whenever the poet had a nervous breakdown.

Over the years Lowell introduced me to other American writers: W.S. Merwin, Stanley Kunitz, Peter Taylor. My friendship with him brought me closer to the America of Nantucket and Boston. And to Russia through the poems we translated into English. One that has endured in my mind, in translation, reflects the fate of poets who, like Mandelstam, had not compromised with the Soviet regime. It is a poem that also speaks of the exiles, though they were less threatened than those who had stayed on in Russia. A poem evocative of my father's unreciprocated loyalty to Russia and to the Russian language: as children, my brother, my cousins, and I were discouraged from speaking French among ourselves, even though we were all attending French schools in France.

> Preserve my words forever for their aftertaste
>   of misfortune and smoke,
> For their tar of collective patience and
>   conscientious work—
> Water in the wells of Novgorod must be black
>   and sweetened
> To reflect a star with seven fins at Christmas.
>
> Oh my Fatherland, my friend, my rough helper,
> Remember your unrecognized brother, the apostate
>   from the people's family—
> I have promised to build you forests of log wells,
> Such as the Tartars built to lower the princes in
>   wooden buckets.

If only your executioners, those frozen blocks,
*   could love me,*
As the Tsar Peter, a deadly marksman, loved the
*   balls he bowled on the lawn—*
For your love, I'll walk through life in an
*   iron shirt,*
For my execution, I'll walk the woods like Peter,
*   and find a handle for the axe.*

For some time in the mid-sixties, Lowell had wanted to go to Russia. I had put him in touch with Nadezhda Mandelstam, with whom he started to correspond: She admired the translations of her husband's poems in *Poets on Street Corners.* She approved unconditionally the notion of free poetic translations as against the literal ones favored in certain academic circles. Lowell hoped to visit her in Moscow. There had been a plan that he, his old school friend Blair Clark, and Senator Eugene McCarthy travel to Russia together. They had asked me to accompany them as an informal guide and interpreter. An American party that would include a distinguished poet and a prominent politician was certain to be closely watched. On the other hand, no member of it was likely to be harassed. By then I was looking for safe ways to go back to Russia. The news that I was working on an anthology that contained the verse of many poets forbidden in Russia, including those of recent Soviet Surrealists and of émigré poets, had been greeted with alarm by the Soviet literary establishment. Possibly it was becoming aware of my activities on behalf of a new generation of dissenting writers and artists.

In early November 1969, I went to New York to apply for a visa and to discuss the Russian trip with Lowell and Blair Clark. It was at that time, when I was staying with the Lowells at their New York apartment, that my host invited me to go with him to Washington, D. C., to participate in a large antiwar demonstration. Until then, my status as a foreigner residing in the United States had kept me from any involvement in American politics. This time, however, after checking with Henry, I decided to go.

We arrived in Washington on an icy, sunny fall afternoon. The capital was already overflowing with marchers. Huge throngs of them, young and old, of every social and ethnic group, filled the airport. Within the city, more were arriving by car, bus, motorcycle, even by bicycle. These were the sixties, and the costumes of the younger demonstrators had an Elizabethan richness—beards, long hair, earrings, tasseled jackets, high boots. Among the older participants, there were impeccably groomed WASPs and tweedy professors with elbow patches and massive horn-rimmed glasses. There were workers, businessmen, housewives, and hippies. People seldom seen together before now gathered in the capital to signal their opposition to the ill-considered, ruthless war in Southeast Asia, which the United States was then escalating.

At the hotel where we were to meet Blair, we ran into Norman Mailer and Dwight Macdonald, the critic. Lowell proposed that we go on the march together. Before setting forth into the crowded streets, we sat in Mailer's room over drinks. Macdonald and Lowell discussed Hertzen's memoirs and the contemporary Russian dissident movement, which was then intensifying. As I listened, I reflected on how much these Americans had come to understand about intellectual life in the USSR since the thaw had set in—and about how much they still did not know. There was a truce in the muted antagonism, which usually hung in the air whenever Mailer and Lowell were in each other's presence.

Soon we set out into the autumn evening filled with demonstrators walking toward Arlington, where the march was to begin. Now the talk was about American politics. Macdonald, wearing a diminutive beret, was as dogmatic and engaging as ever, talking nonstop with erudition, charm, and the stubborn convictions of an old-fashioned radical, an American version of the elderly Russian revolutionaries I had known in childhood. Lowell, with his easy stride, still had the look of a young man, his graying hair closely cropped, the patrician visionary who would astound with his insights into American destiny. Mailer, the pugilist, was in full control of his slugging intellectual incisiveness. All three were taking in the crowd, whose immensity was a source of pride to these early antiwar activists. Now and then, passing students greeted them, usually recognizing Mailer first. Mailer would respond with a gruff but friendly word. All three delighted in being recognized, in their communion with the crowd. This is what political action could accomplish. This new, concerned America was their child. Soon it would force an obtuse government to stop the killings.

I remembered other crowds: the masses of gray-faced Muscovites who every working day jam the sidewalks and subways of the capital, moving in slow, shuffling rivers. But here the marchers were carried along in a huge wave of shared feeling. One lost the sense of one's body, one's ordinary preoccupations, becoming part of an immense, purposeful whole. It was getting dark and very cold as we stood on the bridge linking Arlington to the city. Below the bridge, on a grassy embankment, the headquarters of the march was established, a mass of tents and long makeshift tables. Each marcher was given a slip of paper with a number, the identification number of a GI killed in the war, and a candle to be sheltered inside a paper cup. We were to walk to the Capitol, four miles away, and deposit the numbered slips there, for delivery to the Senate the next day.

As we started moving slowly across the bridge, traffic in the city came to a standstill. The march, which was to last well into the next day, with more marchers arriving during the night and into the morning hours, stretched as far ahead of us as we could see, an endless procession of people walking two and three abreast, carrying candles that flickered in the wind.

I remember the cold, which grew more penetrating as the evening wore on, and the immense avenues dotted with lights. For a long time, as we walked steadily toward it, the illuminated Capitol hung motionless in the night, refusing to grow bigger. Dwight Macdonald, indefatigable and kindly, conversed steadily, sometimes stopping to chop the air with his hands to make a point. Mailer was at his most jovial, delighted to be acknowledged. Lowell, in contrast, talked intently about the dead in Vietnam, the Vietnamese and the Americans, their meaningless numbers. He recalled the poem by Mandelstam we had translated, "Verses about the Unknown Soldier," which, like Akhmatova's *Requiem*, filled Lowell with awe. Randall Jarrell had labored to capture the American war experience, but Mandelstam had created a sweeping evocation of war on a cosmic scale, which, Lowell feared, would soon engulf the planet.

Through the ether measured in decimals,
light-time congeals to one beam,
the numbers grow transparent with pain
a mothlike summation of zeros.

The next day, despite the unrest that was sweeping through the capital, the National Gallery was kept open. Young men and women in bohemian dress rested in the dark grandeur of the columned entrance hall at the top of the stairs. We went in together for a look at the sumptuous lady from Petersburg, Titian's *Venus*, draped in fur and holding a mirror. In the late twenties, this painting had been sold by a Soviet government then in need of Western currency. Before that, it had been my father's favorite painting at the Hermitage.

Lowell was talking enthusiastically about going to Russia. We had to be sure to see the Rembrandts in Leningrad. We would spend as much time as possible visiting Nadezhda Mandelstam. He was becoming slightly infatuated with her as a result of her letters, terse and yet charmingly girlish. Nadezhda Mandelstam wrote in English, a language she had taught for years in Russian provincial universities while eluding the Soviet authorities who had destroyed her husband. As we spoke of Russia, I caught his spirit of optimism.

I returned to Connecticut with renewed energies—and with a new enthusiasm about becoming an American. For some time I had planned to be naturalized, but until now my intention had been motivated solely by practical reasons. Now I looked forward to sharing the nationality of my husband and son and of those thousands I had felt at one with in the capital. But first the trip to Russia lay ahead.

Along with Christmas gifts, I collected medicines and other presents to bring to Russia. I wrote my Moscow acquaintances that I would be coming for a visit with Robert Lowell and a friend of his. Since Senator McCarthy had decided against going to the USSR at that time, the party was to include only three—Lowell, Blair Clark, and myself.

Then, one January morning, less than a week before we were to leave, my travel agent called and in an astonished voice told me that

Mr. Lowell's and Mr. Clark's visas had been issued by the Soviet consulate, but mine had been denied. The agent had queried the Soviet embassy in Washington and learned that the refusal was categorical and not subject to appeal.

CHAPTER TWENTY-TWO

Alexander Solzhenitsyn

The visa refusal might have been linked to *Poets on Street Corners*, the poetry anthology of contemporary Russian verse that had been published in 1968. A full-page, virulent attack against it had been printed in 1969 in the Writers' Union paper, *Literaturnaya Gazeta*. It had been signed by one Pertzov, a minor literary figure said to have been among those who had hounded Mayakovsky before his suicide. I was told that I had briefly become a celebrity in Moscow. Friends there had let me know that, at the time, an attack by Pertzov was regarded as the equivalent of a Pulitzer Prize.

I telephoned Lowell. Indignant upon hearing the news about my visa, he decided on the spot not to go to Moscow. He said he would call Blair Clark. As he hung up, my eye fell on the open suitcase on the floor in a corner of my room. It was ready to be closed, full of treasures—a warm robe for Nadezhda Mandelstam, baby clothes for the newborn Brodsky boy, a book by Salinger for Korney Chukousky.

Sitting on my bed, looking out the window at the birches and the snowy meadows below our Connecticut house, I realized I would not see my Russian friends for a long time. If ever.

In the early sixties, we had left New York City and spent a year and a half in Europe. There Henry started his first novel, *Ilyich Slept Here*, a spoof on Russian-American relations at a time when there were reasons to believe that Russia under Khrushchev was embarked in a slow, hesitant way toward democratization. In France I worked on *Voices in the Snow*, revisiting in spirit not only Pasternak but also those artists still living in Russia—the great Anna Akhmatova, to whom I was introduced by Nadezhda Mandelstam, the poet's widow; Bulat Okudzhava, who became famous as "The Moscow Bard," a Russian Bob Dylan. (He would also write historical novels that illuminated both the past and the forthcoming dark Russian seventies and eighties.); and Bella Akhmadulina, a great beauty, the shining star of her generation of poets. Akhmadulina knew how to remain politically unsoiled; she had a gift for friendships. She is still writing today, still a friend.

As a base in France, we were able to borrow Arnold Fawcus's Boissia, where we had first met and fallen in love. Fawcus, whose press had prospered, now occupied a grander, well-heated chateau in Burgundy which we visited on the way to the Juras. Boissia, full of romantic memories as it was, turned out to be as cold as it had been on that first visit there, but the challenge of working for the first time on books of our own kept us content, as did the proximity to Geneva.

Nearby across the Swiss border my parents, who had moved from New York to Geneva in 1958, sheltered Michael in their comfortable, book-lined new apartment, where we could visit as often as we wished. Whenever we were there Henry and my father played chess after dinner. My parents and I read a lot of newly published Russian poetry to each other. There was a poetic flowering going on in the Soviet Union. I remember my father's excitement when he first came upon Voznesensky's "Goya." Here was a new authentic poetic voice, he reported delightedly. Then little by little *Samizdat* poems smuggled out of Russia became available in the West, including the works of Daniel Andreyev, my father's younger brother, and those of the youthful Joseph Brodsky, and many others. Boissia remained frigid in any season, and Henry and I savored the amenities of Geneva, its cafés, its lakeside beaches. We went to the movies often: this was the era of the great films by Bergman and Fellini.

When I began working on *Poets on Street Corners*, my father was my Russian consultant and Henry, my English one. Henry brilliantly "imitated" poems by Mayakovsky for the collection, but when we tried to translate Pasternak's early autobiography *Safe Conduct*, he balked. It struck him as too eccentric ever to be put into acceptable English—and as far as I know this has proved true to date. But then excitedly we undertook to edit each other's books, something we still do.

Time passed and we were ready to return to the USA. Even before the cruel, divisive Vietnam War broke out, I did not feel in sympathy with many of the policies of the United States government, yet life there with Henry and Michael made more sense to me than the rootlessness of an émigré existence. In any event we had to go back because our money was running out. To support us, Henry would have to take a publishing job in New York.

Fate ruled otherwise. No sooner had we returned to New York than we were invited to spend a weekend with the William Styrons in Roxbury, Connecticut: Michael and their oldest daughter, Susanna, had been friends since infancy. There by chance we were shown a house for sale, on the edge of a grove of birch woods. It was an elegant low-lying redwood house built a few years before. It looked like a California house. Not being a colonial in a town that prized antiques, it was reasonably priced. It had three bedrooms and overlooked a New England meadow worthy of Emily Dickinson, surrounded by wild woods laced with dogwood and wild azaleas.

We both were charmed. It turned out that Henry's father was willing to help us out with the down payment for its purchase. We hoped that our writers' earnings combined would keep us going, and they more or less did. In this poetic setting, Michael went to the old-fashioned local day school, Rumsey Hall. We led a secluded and yet festive existence. These were wonderful years for the three of us, before Michael went away to boarding school. Our literary friendships multiplied despite Roxbury's remoteness. The Arthur Millers, and his wife Inge Morath, Philip Roth, the sculptors Naum Gabo and William Talbot and their families turned out to be country neighbors.

By the late sixties, the Russians kept us very busy; our work on their behalf demanded an ever more secretive way of life. However, until 1969, reporting about Russian literary affairs made it possible for me time and again, to return to the USSR by way of Paris and Geneva on trips that became increasingly more complex and stressful. The liberalization that had been hoped for by Russian experts was not taking place. On the contrary, the Soviet regime was becoming more abusive with each year. My friends in Russia were under ever intensifying police scrutiny. Intimidations and even arrests multiplied, and still they implored me to come back to Moscow with new assignments. Their best hope for survival was recognition in the West. I tried to publicize them with as much tact as I could, through articles in the *New York Times* and books and notably *Poets on Street Corners*. Most of the poems included in this anthology were a revelation for American poetry readers. They spoke of the Russians' thirst for freedom.

Two trips on assignment from the *New York Times*, which I undertook in April and in September of 1967 marked a turning point in our idyllic Connecticut life. As I think of it now, they marked a half-conscious shift in concern. *Poets on Street Corners* was about to be published. I had hoped poems would convey the drama of the contemporary Russian predicament, but it was becoming clear that less allusive denunciations were needed, books that would capture a wider Western public.

On the April trip to Moscow, mutual friends introduced me to Alexander Solzhenitsyn. Within a couple of days I was to meet him, as if by accident, at several gatherings. After a last farewell party—I was leaving the next day—he offered to walk me back to my hotel, through parts of old Moscow that were then being torn down to make way for what is now Kalinin Prospect.

Solzhenitsyn had a commanding, almost military presence, but he was also charming in a somewhat deliberate way. The friends who introduced us were all, without exception, under his spell. Solzhenitsyn must have learned in the labor camps how to put his charm to use. He had the gift of making whomever he was with feel unique—that is, put in his path by a benevolent Providence determined to help him save Russia from her Communist masters. He was surrounded by enthusiastic helpers. Evidently each one felt linked to the writer by a special trust.

I was about to be chosen as one of the helpers. In the dark of night, in an eerie setting of rubble that only a few hours before had been an ancient pink stucco Moscow house, with the dust still hanging in the air, Solzhenitsyn asked me to be his representative for the publication in the United States of one of his books. He told me that it was not *The Cancer Ward,* the novel that likened the USSR to a hospital ward, which was the talk of Moscow at that time— that, he said, he had just given in secret to a visiting Yugoslav journalist.

"The one I'm entrusting to you is a big book—my life," he said. "It must cause a literary explosion." I realized at once that he was referring to the novel brought out of the Soviet Union in the pockets of my father's trench coat in 1965—*The First Circle,* a monumental novel about a secret scientific institute in Stalin's days.

In 1965, my parents, who had been allowed to visit the USSR occasionally since 1957, had stayed in Moscow in connection with my father's literary affairs—two of his works in prose were being published there. At that time Solzhenitsyn came to know them quite well, mainly through the philologist Lev Kopelev, who had been a campmate of Solzhenitsyn's. My parents appeared worthy of Solzhenitsyn's trust. The precious microfilms of *The First Circle* would be kept in the safety of their apartment in Geneva. Ostensibly the microfilms were there for long-term safekeeping, to be released only in the event of the author's death.

"Of course," Solzhenitsyn said as we walked on through the dark streets, "it will all have to be done in the greatest secrecy. You can imagine what would happen to me if you were found out."

Since we had just become acquainted, the mission I was being charged with was clearly a reflection of Solzhenitsyn's high regard for my parents. His confidence may also have been confirmed by mutual friends of Henry's and mine whom he would have consulted independently from one another. For instance, Lev Kopelev and his wife, Raisa, a scholar of American literature, knew about Henry's and my friendships with writers and publishers in the United States. It would be Kopelev, who on my subsequent visit to Moscow, insisted that I take an active role in promoting the author of *One Day* for a Nobel Prize. Kopelev, a generous, expansive man, is portrayed as Rubin in *The First Circle.*

Back in Connecticut, Henry and I spent many days and nights in passionate discussions. The time to awaken the American public to Russian's plight through poems, even though they included Akhmatova's shattering "Requiem," had passed. Henry was convinced that Solzhenitsyn's request presented us with a moral responsibility that was impossible to turn down. In his opinion, only a tightly organized, large-scale Western-style publication—the "explosion" the author had requested—would have a chance of gaining for him the sort of international reputation that might keep him out of prison. We sought counsel from a very few well-informed, trustworthy friends, notably Harrison Salisbury of the *New York Times*.

During my second trip to the USSR in 1967, in the fall of that crucial year, I confirmed in person to Solzhenitsyn our acceptance of his mission. I became Solzhenitsyn's secretly authorized representative in the West for all matters regarding *The First Circle*, under a trusteeship established in Moscow and valid under New York law. In practical terms this meant that I had to put an end to my career as a reporter and commentator on Soviet affairs. After Pertzov's denunciation of *Poets on Street Corners*, I was marked as an adversary of the Communist regime. From now on, saying or writing anything at all on Soviet subjects might bring attention to me and conceivably establish a link with another far more dangerous critic of the regime, Alexander Solzhenitsyn. This is when I started my childhood memoir, *Island in Time*. I also wrote articles on innocuous subjects: Provence, Paris, Nantucket.

In September 1968, the publication of *The First Circle* in the Americas and Europe—coinciding with that of *The Cancer Ward*—made Solzhenitsyn famous throughout the world. Henry's leadership in publishing strategies and his work as editor and translator on *The First Circle* had greatly contributed to this success, and Solzhenitsyn soon afterward entrusted us with the publication of *The Gulag Archipelago*. The previous June, on Trinity Sunday of 1968, at great personal risk, my brother, Sasha, had brought the microfilms of the entire work out of Moscow. In his 1975 memoir, *The Calf and the Oak*, Solzhenitsyn would praise my brother's feat as "the miracle of the Trinity."

Back in January 1968, nine months before Harper & Row's publication of *The First Circle*, Solzhenitsyn instructed us, through my brother, to inform the publisher of the existence of *The Gulag Archipelago* and of our authority to control its eventual publication according to its author's directives. *The Gulag Archipelago*, a multivolume factual exploration of the Soviet penal system, would have to be published within two or three years at most. In the meantime repression was reaching a new intensity in Moscow. Alexander Solzhenitsyn and and the physicist Andrey Sakharov were making history battling the Soviet authorities through open appeals to Western public opinion.

But several years passed and Solzhenitsyn never sent us the agreed-upon signal to bring out *The Gulag Archipelago* in English, though on his orders everything was arranged for its prompt release by Harper & Row. The translation of the first volume was ready. By 1972, Harrison Salisbury was urging me to allow its publication without Solzhenitsyn's signal; at that time, after a series of dramatic confrontations with the authorities, the author appeared to be on the verge of arrest. However, I could not in good conscience bring myself to disobey Solzhenitsyn's specific order. With the continued collaboration of our cotranslator, Thomas Whitney, a close friend of Harrison Salisbury's, with an impressive knowledge of Soviet politics, Henry and I pushed ahead with the translation of the second volume.

At first Solzhenitsyn was elated by the publication—highly publicized, carefully orchestrated with many foreign firms yet with no apparent authorization from him—that *The First Circle* had been given by Harper & Row: it may have helped protect him from the KGB's persecutions and contributed to his nomination for the Nobel Prize. However, for him political and personal pressures were mounting. He had divorced his first wife, accusing her of complicity with the KGB, and had fallen in love with a younger woman, with whom he would have three sons.

In 1970, Alexander Solzhenitsyn was given the Nobel Prize to resounding international acclaim. Some Western critics greeted him as an heir to Tolstoy and Dostoyevsky. The historical significance of his books was recognized in the most diverse quarters. By telling the truth about its penal system, Solzhenitsyn helped destroy the Soviet state; only Andrey Sakharov and Mikhail Gorbachev, each in his own way, would do as much to undermine it. Solzhenitsyn had reaffirmed the power of a writer to change the course of history. Lev Kopelev's dream of glory for the author of *One Day* had been fulfilled.

Little by little, however, a different individual was emerging in place of the intense yet charming novelist I had met at the Kopelevs' in 1967. Solzhenitsyn was now embracing Russian Orthodoxy in earnest and was becoming a stern moralist. His extraordinary accomplishments lent weight to his public utterances on politics, religion, education, and the future of the world threatened by Communism, yet his antiliberal bias surprised many of his admirers, including ourselves. Solzhenitsyn was becoming imperious in his relations with others. As his trustee I had made in his name contractual commitments that he now seemed determined to undo. It was perplexing and indeed frightening in view of the vulnerability of my family and friends within the USSR, and that of his own circle of supporters.

First, he focused his displeasure on the translation of *The Gulag Archipelago*. Bad translations, he complained, undermined his enterprise. More unsettling, he notified us of his displeasure in a note which arrived in Connecticut in October 1972, from a Dr. Heeb, a Swiss lawyer whom Solzhenitsyn had hired to oversee his publishing interests in the West. In the note Solzhenitsyn wrote that he was especially sensitive to English translations, and that he was not pleased with "any of the big translations." It was not a question of author's sensitivity: "on [translation] the whole solidity of my legs depends, and I cannot give in to *anyone* out of good feelings."

At this time Henry and I decided that we had accomplished our mission. *The First Circle* had been published in throughout the West with the "explosion" its author had requested. For us, the time to disengage had come.

It turned out, however, that Solzhenitzyn was unwilling to deal with Harper & Row on the terms he himself had approved. In our family his new communication, dated February 1973 became known as the "Into the Fire" letter. In it the author announced that the fate of *Gulag* must be completely special. The translators would not be chosen by the publishing houses, but in most cases by him personally. The translators would do their work and then, when the job neared completion, *they* [italics mine] would recommend appropriate publishing houses. However, he went on, most publishing houses would cringe at the unusual conditions he would impose, including an extremely small profit margin. "[*Gulag*] will not become a commercial commodity, will not be sold at demented Western prices ($10! This is sixty rubles. This cannot be conceived by our compatriots!")." With obvious relish he predicted that Harper & Row in particular would not like his new conditions.

Then came the astonishing request (in view of Solzhenitzyn's harsh objections to the collaborative translation of the *Gulag* that we had carried forward with Tom Whitney—the same method that had produced the widely praised American edition of *The First Circle*) that I retract my decision to disengage: "I will be sincerely happy if you keep for yourself the right [*sic*] of translation." "If, however, your decision were to be irreversible, then," he concluded, "I see one way of terminating the affair, just for all and offensive to no one: FIRE!"

Evidently, despite our anguished warnings through various messengers, Solzhenitsyn and his lawyer did not comprehend how dangerous it might be for Solzhenitsyn to disregard Harper & Row's rights to *The First Circle* and to *The Gulag Archipelago*. Harper & Row was a commercial concern, with responsibilities to its stockholders. If necessary to protect its right, Harper & Row might be forced to make public what its editors took to be the bona fide legal authority they had received from us to publish the two books. After all, the publishing house had acquired them by paying out faithfully the author's impressive earnings to the bank account established for his benefit.

But to us the most disturbing part of this letter was the word *fire* (*ogon*). When we read it we were amazed. Why burn anything? Mikhail Bulgakov, the author of *The Master and Margarita*, once remarked that "manuscripts do not burn," although of course they have, especially in Russia. We wondered how this instruction could have been written by the man who in *The Gulag Archipelago* describes himself sorrowing on a prison walk on the roof of the Lubyanka as ash falls around him—all that is left of manuscripts that the KGB is burning day and night in the great wave of post–World War II arrests.

We did not realize it when we first received the letter, but in fact it contained the seeds of a deliberate attempt to discredit Henry and me. In the spring of 1975, some months after Solzhenitsyn was forcibly exiled from the Soviet Union, he included the following footnote in the first Russian edition of *The Calf and the Oak*, a lengthy autobiographical work:

Earlier, following immediately after the Russian edition was to appear. I had done everything for it, but two or three dry, mercenary people of Western education turned everything to ashes. . . . The American edition will be late by half a year, will not support me by pulling me across the chasm—and for this reason I think there was the denouement [expulsion]. Yet it would have been, it could have been—conceivably the leaders giving in, if by New Year of the year 1974, all of America was really reading the book, but now in the Kremlin they only know how to weave tales to the effect that it celebrated the Hitlerites. . . .

Evidently Solzhenitsyn felt uncomfortable with the fact that, perhaps to ensure his new family's safety, he had not released the explosive *Gulag Archipelago* in English until exile had caught up with him. Or was the delay an attempt to try to deprive Harper & Row of its rights to the books? Was that why he was blaming the delay on us, mercenary Westerners? I suppose that, to people with a Soviet education, it is known that "mercenary people of Western education" may be vilified and forgotten once they are no longer useful. That was one of Lenin's precepts.

When *The Calf and the Oak* was finally published in the United States, the nameless mercenaries were named. Solzhenitsyn maintained that Henry and I had prevented him from being heard in the West in time, thereby causing him to be exiled from the Soviet Union. We had also prevented the Soviet leaders from acting on his recommendation, spelled out in the 1973 *Letter to the Soviet Leaders*, to replace their Marxist ideology with Russian orthodoxy without necessarily giving up their posts. Even though we did not live in the Soviet Union, Henry and I felt we were caught up in the kind of maneuvering that Soviet officials used to entrap overzealous underlings who showed signs of gaining too much authority.

There were other twists to Solzhenitsyn's vendetta against our family. Soviet kitsch. He and his young wife arrived at my parents' in Geneva with an oversize box of chocolates and a small check to show their appreciation for all that my parents had done for them.

And indeed, beyond their activities as advisors and intermediaries, my mother and father had over the years sent many packages to the Solzhenitsyns—stationery, a tape recorder, baby food for the new-borns, medicines for the adults, colored pencils for a stepson.

That day, along with his thanks, Solzhenitsyn brought a somewhat muffled confirmation of his displeasure with our performance in his service. My father, who greatly admired Alexander Solzhenitsyn for his courage and his literary skills, was too stunned at first to fully comprehend what was happening. He failed to understand Solzhenitsyn's tactic of bringing our participation in his affairs into the open so as to denigrate it in the eyes of the American publishing world—this at considerable risk to those left behind in the Soviet Union. Eventually my father wrote him a letter defending our honor, but on the day this letter reached Solzhenitsyn in Zurich, my father died of sudden heart failure.

My mother received a letter of condolence from Solzhenitsyn. It explained why he had not fully revealed my villainy to my parents when they had last met: "I understood that it would have been painful for you to learn the disagreeable truth, evident to all in America who have had anything to do with this affair."

My mother died shortly afterward. She, who had been so brave as a girl when she was interrogated in the Lubyanka by the notorious Chekist Latsis, and as a young woman under the German occupation, spent the last months of her life in a state of extreme depression. She felt that Solzhenitsyn's behavior toward us had been typical of Soviet tactics: the attempt to create a breach within our family, the innuendos, then the groundless public denunciations. In her mind the ruthless Bolsheviks had once again overwhelmed the naive Socialist Revolutionaries, whom they had duped in October 1917, and succeeded in fairly eradicating from the face of the earth. She died believing that after six decades of Communism there was no hope for Russia.

In the late seventies I recorded whatever could be told at that time of our six-year involvement. *Solzhenitsyn and the Secret Circle*—eventually serialized in the Moscow literary journal *Voprosy Literatury*—is about the group of friends in and outside of Russia who helped Alexander Solzhenitzyn to be published abroad. As I wrote this book I was looking for an explanation to Solzhenitsyn's aggressiveness toward those who had tried to help him over the years. On that subject in 1978, George Kennan wrote a letter that helped mitigate the sadness I felt at that time:

> What you ran across, in your effort to be of help to Solzhenitsyn, was something that has impressed itself on me in many ways over the years and has affected my thinking about Russia quite strongly: and this is the extraordinary lack of tolerance and common charity in the Russian political mentality, not only, unfortunately, in the Bolshevik, or radical-socialist mentality, but pretty much across the board; with it, the capacity for a total, heartless rejection of anyone who does not share one's own orientation and outlook; and with it, finally, a tendency to be as unfeeling in one's attitude towards the individual man as one is solicitous (or claims to be) for the fate of man in the mass. . . . In the case of Solzhenitsyn this is compounded, surely, and understandably so, by the coarsening and primitivizing of the Russian character produced by sixty years of Soviet rule.

Henry and I survived our involvement with the author of *The Gulag Archipelago*. We moved away from the house in Connecticut, where we had worked on his manuscripts and conducted his affairs, settling in San Francisco. There, upon learning that Alexander Solzenitsyn intended to publish fresh disparagements of our activities on his behalf, we filed a lawsuit against him in order to ward off further attacks.

The First Amendment shielded Solzhenitsyn from liability for his published denunciation, but to date our suit has achieved its purpose. We were never again slandered by him in print. At that time I gave up any thought of ever going back to Russia, and indeed for two decades was officially unwelcome there. Mercifully, my relatives in the USSR were left alone: evidently the KGB never probed in depth our connection to Solzhenitsyn.

CHAPTER TWENTY-THREE

Far from Russia

In 1945, when I was fifteen, we had returned to Paris from the island of Oléron after a five-year absence. I was home at last in my native city. That memorable summer was hot and dry. I remember a sense of euphoria. The seemingly endless nightmare had ended. My father, a member of the French Resistance on Oléron, had been arrested by the Germans but had been released unharmed; he had not been deported. By the time of his arrest, shipments of French prisoners to Poland and Germany had stopped as a result of the Allies' blanket bombardments of railway centers in occupied Europe. That fall he had found a job in Paris in the film industry, which had not yet collapsed in the French postwar depression.

We moved back into our apartment in Le Plessis near Paris, which, as if by magic, had been untouched throughout the war years. We found it as we had left it five years before, not an object missing—our extremely modest possessions were left alone. My father's notebooks lay on his desk, where he had last put them down in 1939. My grade school manuals were still on their shelf, my mother's knitting in a basket next to them. A layer of dust covered everything. It was an odd, unforgettable homecoming.

Life resumed happily around the oval dining table with the pale yellow and green oilcloth on which stood bouquets arranged by my mother. In most ways things picked up where they had stopped in 1939: I had not forgotten the apache of my childhood, nor given up the hope of meeting him one day. I got ready for the approaching school year and helped my mother organize our daily life for the coming winter. We needed to register for ration cards; somehow, somewhere, to locate a stove, since central heating no longer functioned in the apartment; make contacts with friends and relatives we hadn't seen in five years.

My euphoria proved shortlived: the Allies' victory over the Germans had reawakened my father's fierce desire to live in Russia, which he had been forced to leave at sixteen. It turned out that, right after the war, there was an interlude, about a year or two, during which Stalin decreed that citizenship and return visas be granted to all Russian émigrés in France, including individuals like my parents, who had until then been systematically denied the right to go home after the revolution. Everyone of Russian origin was invited to register at the Soviet Embassy. We had no idea of it then, but evidently the KGB was establishing exhaustive lists of Russians living abroad.

My father, who had fought in the French underground alongside a group of patriotically minded Russians brought out to Oléron as prisoners of war, could not imagine that, in the Soviet Union, the Great Terror had not ended. His Russian companions in arms, absorbed in sabotage activities against the Germans, had somehow failed to tell him that, on Stalin's orders, the secret police were as fearsome as ever, even as the Soviet Union was engulfed in war. It was not that these men, who were in a frenzy of hatred against the Germans, had deliberately lied. For rank-and-file Soviet citizens after thirty years of Marxist indoctrination, the line between historical fact and wishful thinking was blurred.

Indeed, the conditions under which these soldiers had survived German POW camps in the Ukraine had been atrocious beyond one's wildest imaginings. They were still in a state of shock. A visceral fidelity to Russia was their only beacon. To them my father was a fairy tale incarnation of what Russia might have been, had the country's politics taken a different turn in 1918. They instinctively wanted to ignore the fact that my father was an endangered survivor from a gigantic cataclysm, that his presence on Oléron was accidental, that he was in no way signaling the emergence of a better Russia born out of her sufferings.

Though the end of the war made their return to Russia imminent, when we said good-bye our new friends could not bring themselves to confront the prospect that, as former war prisoners of the Germans, they would not be welcomed in the Soviet Union. No one wanted to think that, after all the Soviet people had endured, it would be further punished by an aging, demented tyrant. In our remote corner of France, on Ile d'Oléron, which for us had been a providential island in time, this was particularly hard to believe.

Now in Le Plessis my father was making plans to take the four of us to Moscow. My eight-year-old brother, Sasha, was enchanted. He was convinced that in the Soviet Union everyone would be as nice as the Russian soldiers on Oléron, much nicer than the dour working-class French people who were our neighbors in Le Plessis. My mother was troubled but resigned in the face of my father's determination. A victim of the Cheka's onslaught against fellow Socialists during the Revolution, she knew how traitorous the Bolsheviks were. She hated them and yet part of her wanted to share in my father's dream. As for myself, I was horrified. After what felt like a lifetime away from Paris, all I wanted to do was to live out my life there as an ordinary Parisian.

The intensity of my father's yearning was awesome. Above all he wished to be reunited with his beloved younger brother, Daniel. In Russia he would at last be able to lead "a life useful to her people," as he put it—a phrase that I found particularly irksome, though it was totally sincere. That we were without news from close friends who had gone off to the Soviet Union before the war was blamed on the disruptions caused by the war, which had ravaged that country. Had we not had a letter from Daniel?

Before the war, before we had found ourselves on Oléron, my uncle Daniel had made his presence felt in our small apartment in Le Plessis. No less enigmatic than my grandfather, whose somber-looking self-portraits had fascinated me as a child, my uncle in his one photograph in my father's study appeared lighthearted, almost cheerful. He lived in Moscow, and he and my father had been separated since early childhood. Despite this separation, which my father considered catastrophic, or perhaps because of it, he felt a mystical connection between himself and his younger brother. In 1906, when he was only three, Daniel's birth had caused the death of their mother, Alexandra Mikhailovna, Leonid Andreyev's first wife. For my father, Daniel was the one remaining link with a mother whose absence haunted him all his life.

In the fall of 1945, some weeks after our return to Le Plessis, a letter from my uncle arrived. I was about to start classes at Marie-Curie, a beautiful, newly built lycée some forty minutes' walk from our apartment. I had been filled with a mixture of apprehension and delight. For lack of a school on Oléron, I had had no formal classes of any kind for three years. Now, wondrously, the Allies had won the war, and I would be going to a prestigious, progressive lycée. I would be with girls of my age, studying all sorts of enticing subjects—history, English, French literature. On Sundays I would explore Paris and go to the Louvre and to the Cluny Museum and make friends of my own age.

My uncle's letter had come in response to a note from my father, delivered to Daniel in Moscow by Ivan Maksimovich Fitukov, one of the Soviet soldiers on his way home from Oléron to the Ukraine. This letter spoke of the deaths, during the war, of several much-loved relatives, including the aunt and uncle who had brought him up after his mother's death, when as a small child he was taken away from his father's mansion in Finland. In his letter, my uncle announced his recent marriage to a young painter, Alla, with whom he was deeply in love.

For a time some of the mysteries surrounding Daniel's existence appeared dispelled. He had come back from the war, he was living again in the old family apartment in Moscow, he was writing letters. And he loved my father no less than my father loved him:

> ...My beloved brother,
>
> At last I know that you are all alive and well. For eight years I had no news whatever of you. Though I never lost the inner conviction that you and your family would survive, there were good reasons for anxiety. I learned of your work in the Resistance with joy—you and I fought a common enemy on opposite ends of Europe....
>
> I spent a long time at the front, first in the defense of Moscow and then of Leningrad during the blockade. I

reached Leningrad by way of frozen Lake Ladoga, the one road that was open at that time. Later I was transferred to Veliky Luk and Nevel, and then to Latvia. The war has left me shattered physically and psychologically. Even before it ended I was hospitalized. But full recovery is impossible. . . .

We lead a very quiet life, Alla and I. We sometimes go to a concert and, very rarely, to a play. We look forward immensely to your return home and to starting life in common—what could be better?

My beloved brother, there are no words to express how dearly I love you, how I miss you, how much your family means to me, how we both look forward to embracing you and the two Olgas and small Sasha.

Iv. Maks. sends his regards,

Your brother, Daniel

Encoded in this fraternal letter there was a future of disasters for Daniel and his wife and their circle of friends. "Iv. Maks." referred to Fitukov, the Russian soldier from Oléron, an endearing, courageous peasant reminiscent of Platon Korotayev in *War and Peace*. We would not know this for another twelve years, but as soon as Ivan Maksimovich reached his native village, he was accused by the KGB of plotting Stalin's assassination—together with my father. Ivan Maksimovich was arrested and sent to the Gulag in Siberia. A similar fate befell the Russian exiles who returned to the USSR in those years, whether they were old émigrés or people recently displaced as a result of the war, like the Soviet soldiers who had worked for the French Resistance on Oléron.

However, my father, who was not to know about these arrests for decades, was elated by Daniel's letter—his dream of a Russian homecoming was about to be fulfilled. But I thought that it was all terribly wrong, and not only because I wanted to live peaceably in peacetime Paris. I was certain of it. It should have been evident to anyone with a sober mind: were we to go to Russia, the four of us, we would be arrested. Information about the monstrous scope of the Soviet Gulag was beginning to seep into the West, although it was dismissed in the liberal French press as malevolent, lunatic anti-Soviet propaganda—the Soviets' powers of deception were huge.

In the French newspapers of that time, acrimonious debates about was truly happening in the Soviet Union were the order of the day. Tales of Russian heroism during the war dimmed the memories of the great Moscow trials, which, only a few years before, had awakened public opinion to the reality of systematic terror throughout the Soviet empire. They also dimmed the impact of reports about the immediate situation, which was unspeakably cruel to millions of Soviet citizens.

My father and I had a number of tempestuous scenes, something we never had had before. It seemed evident that both my father's background as the son of a writer who had vehemently and very publicly denounced Lenin's rise, and my mother's, whose adoptive father had been Lenin's Socialist archrival before the Bolshevik coup d'état in 1917, would have doomed us had we gone to Russia. I told my father that he was blind, that there was undeniable evidence of relentless Communist persecutions in the USSR. My parents could do as they pleased, but I would not go to Moscow, I said, certainly not right away. Until the completion of my lycée education, which would take three years at least, I would live with my Aunt Natasha in nearby Cachan.

My father was thunderstruck. We were so close, we understood each other so well in so many ways, and yet I was interfering with what he considered as the sacred, ultimate goal of his life—rejoining his people, putting himself at Russia's service. But he also realized that my mother, silent as she was, could not bear the prospect of breaking up our family, even for a time. As a rare survivor of the hundreds of thousands of fellow Socialists killed off by the Bolsheviks over the decades, she knew what separations of this kind usually meant. Deeply upset, my father nonetheless gave in to us. My parents and Sasha would not leave for the USSR for a year or two, long enough to give me time to settle in at Marie-Curie and learn to be independent.

However, the practical aspects of the projected return to Russia remained vague. After the war in ruined France, the mere matter of procuring enough food each day so as to stay alive took enormous amounts of time and energy. For several years, while my father commuted to his faraway job as a film editor and Sasha and I went to school, this was my mother's chief occupation. Under these circumstances, to arrange for a journey to a distant land for a family of four was a daunting enterprise, although I remember my mother trying to collect warm clothing for the voyage.

One cold, gray day the following winter, a postcard from Daniel arrived in Le Plessis. I still recall the late afternoon when I returned from the lycée and found my mother in a state of extreme agitation—relief for the sake of our immediate future, and grief for my father who had not yet come home from work and who was certain to be crushed. My uncle wrote that he'd be delighted to see us—just as soon as I had graduated from the Sorbonne. Now there was no doubt. Daniel knew exactly my age. He was telling us not to come to the USSR at this time.

Some months after Daniel's postcard reached us, the Soviet authorities stopped granting automatic entry visas to Russians abroad. Perhaps the glut of new arrivals being processed into the Gulag caused this change in policy? Alexander Solzhenitsyn in his *Gulag Archipelago* suggests that Stalin had begun to fear the enthusiastic reports about foreign lands, which the returning Russians brought back with them: these belied the strident Soviet propaganda about the social and political evils of the West.

Little by little life in Le Plessis became easier. Paris was a marvelous place to be after the war. Russian émigré literary life was reviving, yet there is no question that for himself if not for the four of us, my father would have preferred martyrdom in Russia to safety in France.

CHAPTER TWENTY-FOUR

My Uncle Daniel Andreyev

My uncle Daniel Andreyev's fate turned out to have been tragic beyond the imagination of those who lived in the relative safety of emigration. His ordeals turned a good classical poet with a traditional Russian Orthodox sensibility into a poet-visionary in the tradition of William Blake or St. John of the Cross. World War II had been the first trial for the pacifist Daniel, though he was allowed to serve in it primarily as an orderly, taking care of the wounded and burying the dead. The poems he wrote about the war are solemn and stark. Here is a fragment about the lifting of the siege of Leningrad, in which Daniel participated. He had reached the expiring city by way of the ice road across Lake Ladoga:

> *Night winds! Dark mountain skies*
> *Over the snowy grave of Leningrad,*
> *You were our trial and our prize.*

> *Today I treasure like a relic*
> *What I remember of that night*
> *When stubbornly I marched*
> *Together with the Russian people*
> *Somber then, covered to its eyes with steel.*

> *From the hills of Moscow,*
> *The steppes of Saratov*
> *Where waves of rye shine in the summer,*

From the northern taiga where ancient
Cedars howl deeply in the wind.

All races welded into one
For a bitter military deed
—One long live rope on the black ice.

Daniel's next trial came in early 1947, most probably a conse-
quence of the message sent to him by my father through Ivan Maksimovich Fitukov. In any case, Daniel would have already been
suspect; he was known to be working on a novel about Moscow
intellectuals after the Revolution. One evening he gave a reading
from his novel *Voyagers of the Night*, to a group of friends, and one
of them denounced him to the authorities. Daniel and everyone who
attended the reading, about thirty people in all, were arrested, including his wife, Alla. They were accused of taking part in a plot
to kill Stalin, masterminded from Paris by my father.

Alla and Daniel were interrogated and tortured for more than a
year. No one was shot; in a show of humanitarian make-believe, the
death penalty had been officially outlawed in the Soviet Union after
the war. Daniel was sentenced to twenty-five years in prison and
Alla to twenty-five years in labor camp, while the circle of people
implicated in the imaginary plot against Stalin continued to grow
and arrests multiplied. *Voyagers of the Night* was lost forever. The KGB
destroyed the one existing copy of the novel. Long afterward in the
sixties in Moscow it was said by survivors of this case that Alla had
fallen under the spell of her interrogator and given him names of
alleged conspirators. My parents maintained that along with her
great qualities, and notably the persistence with which she preserved
her husband's oeuvre, Alla has an exalted, somewhat unstable personality. This she herself acknowledges in an autobiography recently
published in Moscow.

Daniel's fate took a fantastic turn after his arrest. Incarcerated
for almost ten years in the sinister prison in the medieval town of
Vladimir, my uncle escaped from it in spirit—by becoming a mystic
poet. Because of his meek, almost saintly disposition, even his jailers
helped him at times, allowing him to hide the scraps of paper on
which he wrote his poems. One of these, composed earlier, in 1937,

was prophetic of what would be Daniel's earthly as well as his spiritual road—there is no better way to explain how the Russian psyche survived decades of terror. Its last line is remembered in Russia:

No one will find you on your soul's high sea.

After Stalin's death, Alla and Daniel were released—she in 1956, he in 1957. While still in prison my uncle had suffered a heart attack. He had been made to walk up stairs right afterward—up the stone stairs of the Vladimir prison—and this had been his death warrant. In freedom he lived on for only a year and a half. Yet with his wife's help he was able to transcribe almost eight hundred pages of his works, which were preserved through a truly extraordinary occurrence. When Daniel was released, the director of the Vladimir prison let Alla take out Daniel's belongings without searching them. Daniel's poetic and philosophic lifework was saved.

Daniel Andreyev's legacy is made up of whole cycles of poems as well as monumental, elaborate philosophical treatises, including a cosmology he called *The Rose of the World*, which is a best-seller in Russia today. His *Iron Mystery*, inspired by the medieval European mystery plays, is a masterful polyphonic creation, a symbolist's conception of the universe in which harmony is established after a series of cosmic upheavals. Today Daniel Andreyev is celebrated in Russia, where mysticism is part of the post-Soviet sensibility. For a certain kind of modern Russian truth seeker, his works are more satisfying than Leonid Andreyev's, who offered no definitive answers to life's mysteries. Daniel on the other hand presents an infinitely complex, hierarchic vision of the cosmos, which has a logic of its own.

Now in the nineties I read the letters my uncle Daniel wrote to my father, preparing them for publication in a Petersburg journal whose name would have pleased him, *Zvezda*, "Star." I am writing the forward to these letters directly in Russian. Last summer, among my mother's papers left unsorted since her death in 1979, I found a small packet of yellowed letters in a manila envelope. My uncle Daniel was a very brave man. I had not realized that so many of his letters written during the various stages of the Terror were sent through the mail, in an era when contact with the West was as a rule a mortal danger for Soviet citizens.

My father's letters to his brother have not been preserved. All of my uncle's papers, including his father's letters, were destroyed when he and his wife were arrested. Even by Stalinist standards, the destruction of originals by Leonid Andreyev, a famous writer, a friend of Maxim Gorky and of Tolstoy seems exceptional. In fact Andreyev's books were not reprinted for decades despite his celebrated early friendship with Gorky, the future inventor of Socialist Realism, a writer who would eventually be seduced and ruthlessly exploited by Stalin for many years—from 1928 until his death in 1935, when Stalin staged a colossal propaganda-laden state funeral to mark his death.

My uncle's letters to my parents are open and joyous, full of haunting descriptions of Russian landscapes. Like my father, Daniel was enamored of the natural world—and especially of the forests and rivers and meadows of central Russia. The letters are overflowing with a desire to alleviate my father's anguish and help him accept his exile, at least temporarily. Expressed in many of his poems, my father's sorrow had something of Ovid's bitterness at not being allowed to go home. Exile is a wound that nothing will heal. Once, early in 1923 or 1924—the letter is not dated—Daniel obliquely reveals his wish to join my father in Paris. However, at that time it cost an exorbitant sum to secure an exit visa from the Soviet Union, and neither brother can hope to raise it. In 1927, my uncle rejoices in my parents' wedding and later in my birth and that of Sasha.

There is a letter to me when I was seven years old, written in carefully drawn block letters, about my drawings of the Knights of the Round Table. Daniel was then deeply involved with the legend of the Holy Grail. Which is my favorite knight, he asks, is it Lancelot or Perceval? Or Sir Owen? At about the same time he tells us that he has started a novel, writing and rewriting it painstakingly—the first versions of the lost *Voyagers of the Night*.

In the twenties, Daniel's longing for my father's return to Russia is no less intense than my father's own. The sons of a celebrated writer, who was clairvoyant and self-centered, have a visceral need for each other. In the early thirties, still believing in the imminence of my father's arrival in Moscow, Daniel seems oblivious to the attention he must be attracting on the part of the authorities as he undertakes a variety of steps in the hope of furthering his brother's homecoming.

Daniel asks his godfather, Maxim Gorky, to intervene with Stalin—but Gorky dies just then, most probably assassinated by Stalin, and his intervention with the dictator remains unrecorded. Then a few weeks later, he offers to write a letter to Stalin. Against his better judgment because he is aware of Isaac Babel's growing political vulnerability, he will try to get in touch with this remarkable writer who is about to be arrested and killed in the most horrific manner— all this in the hope of obtaining Soviet visas for the four of us— in 1937, at the height of the Great Terror!

Judging by Daniel's letters, at first he does not fully comprehend that he lives at a time when the Devil has come to Moscow, as one of his literary elders, Mikhail Bulgakov, would have it. In the midst of his adoring adoptive family, he leads a sheltered life. At thirty he is already an exacting poet. A few of his poems, those of a very young man, are included in a letter from 1938. That same year, a ten-page letter contains a critique of some of my father's early verse. Then suddenly there is a rumpled note from 1939, apparently delivered through a third party, which puts an end to all communication between the brothers for years, until that postwar letter welcoming us to Moscow. Here is the 1939 note:

> Dearest Dimushka,
>
> We are all alive and well, more or less. I think of you often, very often, beloved ones, who though far away are dear to my heart. It is sad that things turned out as they did, but it is for the best. My wish is that you'd find joy and meaning in that life that fate has assigned you. I embrace you and Olga and the children. Though our address hasn't changed, there is no need to reply.
>
> Your loving D.

This spring with the help of one of my nieces, a Russian scholar who helps me decipher Daniel's handwriting, which resembles closely my father's and Leonid Andreyev's, I read and reread my uncle's letters. His is an enchanting, giving personality. He is brilliant. However, unlike the rest of our Russian-Parisian family, Daniel does not like Pasternak's poetry. This is my only slight disappointment at this unexpected encounter with my uncle and my father and with a forgotten part of myself. I remember now that as a child I thought that perhaps my uncle was a victim of that same evil force that stood for so long in the way of the seekers of the Holy Grail. Why otherwise would he not come to be with us in Le Plessis?

In 1997, on a visit to my brother, Sasha, who lives in Paris and works for UNESCO, I ask him whether he recalls conversations about Daniel in the postwar years when we were without news of him—1947, 1948, 1949, 1950, 1951—the year of my marriage to Henry—1952, 1953, 1954, 1955, 1956, 1957, when after an exile of forty years my father was at last given a visitor's visa to Russia and he, my mother, and Sasha went to Moscow and met Daniel some months before his death. Sasha says, "No, as far as I remember, we didn't say anything at all about Daniel. Not for years, not after that shattering postcard about the need for you to finish your Sorbonne education. It was as if he was living in heaven, and we could not reach him for that reason."

"Perhaps we did not want to acknowledge that Daniel might be dead," I say.

"No, somehow I think that we always knew that Daniel was alive—somewhere," says Sasha. "It's just that we did not want to imagine where he might be. Was it perhaps some sort of superstition? Or is it that the Soviet system mandated people not to ask questions?

"Remember," Sasha adds, "despite all that was revealed, even when Mother and Vadim and I met with Daniel in 1957 and heard of his ten years in the Vladimir prison, Vadim would still not fully comprehend what was happening in the Soviet Union—not until Solzhenitsyn's *Ivan Denisovich* was published and he saw the truth at last, as did thousands of other Western liberals. It is Solzhenitsyn's great feat to have found the words with which to awaken them. Thirty years after the Great Purges, public opinion was at last ready to see what Communism had done to Russia."

CHAPTER TWENTY-FIVE

Homecoming

My father often said that it was not he who had left Russia, that it had been Russia who left him. When his father died in Finland in 1919, sixteen-year-old Vadim found himself beyond the newly drawn Soviet border, unable to join Daniel and his maternal family in Moscow. Unwilling to stay on in Finland, he decided instead to take part in the civil war between the Reds and the Whites, whose murderous battles were then at their height. A very long, adventurous journey took my father from Finland to Georgia, which had not yet fallen to the Bolsheviks.

My father never forgot the last stand against the Bolsheviks in the Caucasus mountains—there in the nineties in Dagestan, the fate of Russia is played out once again:

> *Thus it was and will be again—*
> *Gunshots and the murmur of nightingales*
> *The soul will die but it will not forget,*
> *You are the light, you are my youth.*

When the moderate Georgian Socialists on whose side he fought were finally defeated by the Bolsheviks, my father, along with several hundred thousand people who had opposed Lenin, were evacuated from the southern reaches of Russia to Constantinople. After some months he found himself in Berlin. There a lively Russian literary life had migrated from the ever more repressive Soviet Union. Pas-

ternak and Mayakovsky were staying in Berlin at that time, as well
as were a number of younger Russian writers with whom my father
formed friendships. By the mid-twenties these people either went to
Paris or to Berlin, where a new German state was being born. Others
returned to the Soviet Union; most of them perished sooner or later
at the hands of the secret police.

In the twenties and thirties Paris was a harsh city for Russian
émigrés, but it was possible for them to survive there. My father
married into the Chernov clan led by my grandmother Olga Kol-
bassin Chernov, a talented journalist who had three beautiful daughters and a rare gift for making daily life festive. Literary friendships
abounded. The well-known émigré Symbolist Alexey Remizov was
my godfather.

There were painters too among our family friends. I was taken
as a child to the studios of Alexander Exter and of Natalia Gon-
charova. That both artists were women who were well-known made
it even more mesmerizing. The smell of turpentine, the sight of
pencils and pastels, "which were for the grown-ups only" entranced
me. At that time my father started buying tinted Canson paper for
me to draw on. This was a luxury that flattered and inspired me.
On special occasions my mother and my aunts would let me use
the pastels out of their outsize Sennelier box.

In the thirties, despite the grueling work he had to do to support
us—he was first a linotypist, then a film editor—my father wrote
a memoir that earned him critical acclaim, notably that of Vladimir
Nabokov. Called *Detstvo* (*Childhood*) it was printed in the leading
liberal émigré journal published in Paris in the thirties. *Detstvo* was
published in book form in Moscow much later during the Khrushchev thaw thanks to Korney Chukovsky, a protegé of Leonid
Andreyev who was a popular children's author and a literary critic
before he was censored by the Communist leadership. *Detstvo*
charmed Russian readers and went through several printings. It was
speaking to them from that other, tantalizing world, the forbidden
world of the Paris emigration. Today at Moscow University this
book is on the reading list in a graduate sociology class, helping
illustrate the values of a vanished Russian intelligentsia before the
revolution.

Detstvo gives the reader a memorable portrait of Leonid Andreyev.

It is about my father's relationship with his celebrated father, whom he worshiped at a distance. It is elegant and restrained and absolutely honest. Through the eyes of an adolescent, it gives us a glimpse of the fabulous first decade of the twentieth century in Russia and of the oncoming revolution, with which, in the words of Anna Akhmatova, the true twentieth century began. Shortly before the Brezhnev Era of Stagnation set in, two other works in prose by my father were published in Russia. A few poems appeared in the journal *Zvezda*. My father came home to Russia through his books, and this illuminated the end of his life.

In 1960, when I first went to Russia under the sign of Boris Pasternak, Daniel Andreyev, who had died the previous year, was never openly discussed anywhere. He was considered an enemy of the people. So was Pasternak, but echoes of the fracas surrounding the successful publication abroad of *Doctor Zhivago* had penetrated the Iron Curtain. From his literary beginnings before the revolution, Pasternak the modernist had been worshiped by a small literary elite. Unlike Leonid Andreyev, whose books were beginning to be reissued, or Pasternak whose early editions were passed from hand to hand, Daniel's works existed only in manuscripts, which his widow went to great pains to hide. Today they are published in printings of tens of thousands.

Little by little, my parents, my brother, and I smuggled copies of his texts out to the West. We admired Daniel's poems and we shared them with other lovers of Russian poetry. We pondered his visions, mixing Russian history and Hinduism—they are not unlike a version of Peter Brooks's *Mahabharata* that might have been created by a Russian mystic. However, it would have been unwise to try to publish Daniel's writings in the West in those years: their dissemination could have been fateful for his widow.

In 1989, on my way to Moscow from San Francisco after more than twenty years of Brezhnev's repression, during which the Soviet authorities had kept me out of Russia, I had a moving encounter with my uncle during a stopover in Paris. In the company of Olivier Pagès, as interested in ancient architecture as ever, I had gone to Editeurs Réunis, a Russian bookstore on rue de la Montagne-Sainte-Geneviève, near the Panthéon. It is located next door to the café where Henry had proposed to me. The hotel where my father had lived just before he married my mother is around the corner, but that day I was not looking for sentimental lore. I was preparing myself for my forthcoming trip to Russia, the first in two decades. I wanted to buy some of Solzhenitsyn's books about the Russian Revolution, while Olivier leafed through stacks of albums about Russian medieval cities—Yaroslavl, Suzdal, Vladimir.

As Olivier and I were leaving the bookstore I noticed high on a shelf a brooding, beautiful man's face on the cover of a volume propped upright. I thought to myself, "How strange, a portrait of Baudelaire I have never seen." We stepped outside, but on an impulse I went back in. I wanted to look again at that man's face. Standing on tiptoe, I reached for the volume and looked at its cover. It was oddly familiar. When I opened the book I saw that it was a selection of Daniel Andreyev's poems, published for the first time in Moscow some weeks before. Seeing my uncle's face and holding his book of poems were a sign, the kind of vindication I had sought in the artists' lofts of my youth, and again in the late fifties at the age of thirty, when I went to Russia for the first time and met Pasternak at his home.

I will never forget that sunny late morning in the Russian countryside of Peredelkino in January 1960, a few months before Pasternak died. The sparkling snow, the fir trees, the half-torn note pinned to the door on the veranda at the side of the house: "I am working now. I cannot receive anybody. Please go away." On an impulse, thinking of the small gifts I was bringing the poet from admirers in the West, I did knock. The door opened.

Pasternak stood there, wearing an astrakhan hat. When I introduced myself he welcomed me cordially as my father's daughter—they had met in Berlin in the twenties and again in the late fifties. Pasternak's speaking voice was like his poems. In an instant the warm, slightly nasal singsong voice assured me that my parents' country still existed and that it had a future as real as that sunny day. Today, no matter how harsh life in Russia is, that flash of feeling is proved true. Russia lives on, and the natural world around us which Pasternak celebrated, though threatened, is still as magnificent as ever, and it is mine to paint.